BELIEVE IT!

CHICAGO CUBS
2016 WORLD SERIES
CHAMPIONS

CHICAGO SUN⊙TIMES

Jim Kirk, Editor and Publisher

Chris Fusco, Managing Editor

Chris De Luca, Deputy Managing Editor, News and Sports

Jeff Agrest, Deputy Sports Editor

Albert Dickens, Sports Assistant

Copy/Design Desk
Matt Corradino, Rob Hollingsworth, Bob Mazzoni, Humberto Perez,
Dennis Sabo, John Silver and James Smith

Reporters
Steve Greenberg, Daryl Van Schouwen and Gordon Wittenmyer

Columnists
Rick Morrissey and Rick Telander

This book contains content published in The Chicago Sun Times and on chicago.suntimes.com during the 2016 MLB season. Dates on stories reflect publication dates on chicago.suntimes.com.

Peter J. Clark, Publisher
Nicky Brillowski, Book and Cover Design

ISBN: 978-1-940056-43-2 (paperback)
ISBN: 978-1-940056-41-8 (hardcover)

Printed in the United States of America
KCI Sports Publishing   3340 Whiting Avenue, Suite 5   Stevens Point, WI 54481
Phone: 1-800-697-3756   Fax: 715-344-2668
www.kcisports.com

Contents

This one is for Ronnie and Ernie and Milt and Gentleman Jim and all the departed Cub souls of yore who never saw it happen.

It's for the current players and their families and Cubs management and can-eating goats everywhere.

It's for executive chairman Tom Ricketts, who walked through the upper deck on the night the Cubs won the pennant and was mobbed with joyful high fives as he moved along.

But most of all, it's for Cubs fans here and beyond, the ones on this earth, up in the air, out in the ether, in family rooms, sick rooms, the living and the spirits who waited 71 years for their beloved team to make it once more into the World Series.

Ding-dong, the witch is dead!

The Cubs have won the World Series, moving to a place they haven't been since 1908.

A World Series crown? We'll get to that after this feat sinks in.

Yes, you have suffered Indians fans, and welcome to the final showdown. But the Cubs have suffered more. And their fans most of all.

Now we can say it: Mission accomplished.

It's impossible to look at the Cubs future without drifting into the past. Call it sentiment, call it shared yearning, call it the bonding of so many years.

But those hard-luck 1969 Cubs with Fergie Jenkins and Ron Santo and Ernie Banks, Billy Williams, Glenn Beckert, Randy Hundley, Don Kessinger – this is for them. Even for Don Young.

This is for the 1984 Cubs of Rick Sutcliffe, Bobby Dernier, Jody Davis and Steve Trout, who had their hearts cruelly broken by the Padres in the NLCS. This is for Leon Durham. That ball that went between your legs? Forget about it!

This is for the 1989 Cubs and the 1998 Cubs, and, of course, the 2003 Cubs of Mark Prior, Kerry Wood, Sammy Sosa, et al. – the "five outs away" team. That's all gone. All washed away.

"Shout," that joyous gospel/rock tune came blasting out of the PA before the Cubs started batting in the eighth inning. The fans sang along and the stadium swayed. That's a scary feeling, people, an ancient structure like this rocking from delirium.

Before the ninth inning Eminem shouted defiantly: "The music, the moment, you own it!' and again the building quaked.

The last out came and the Cubs' gloves went flying into the air in ecstasy.

As the Cubs ran around the field in joy, it was just a shocking sight. It's just hard to believe. You know what I mean.

This one goes out to lifetime fan Bill Murray. It goes out to Steve Goodman, the troubadour who died young, and, like the rest of us, never knew Cubs success. It goes out to his family and his late mom, Minnette, the 4-9, 90-pound dynamo who was as sweet and spirited as any Cubs fan anywhere.

It's there for the 2007 and 2008 Cubs, great teams that couldn't make it out of the first round.

As everybody sang "Go, Cub, Go," Goodman's anthem to possibility, sang it once, then sang it again after the trophy presentation, and the white "W" flags flew, it was, indeed – at last – all good.■

After Winning Winter, Cubs Start Trying To Win October

Cubs starting pitchers Jon Lester and John Lackey run sprints with teammates during spring training. *AP Photo*

by GORDON WITTENMYER

That the Cubs will carry a target on their backs every time they take the field this year is clear to everyone from the clubhouse to front office, a challenge manager Joe Maddon plans to "embrace."

But the biggest fight the Cubs might have on their hands as spring training opens this week is the sheer magnitude of expectations inside and outside the organization after winning 97 games, beating the Pirates and Cardinals in the playoffs and then pulling off $276 million of acquisitions that have made the Cubs America's favorites to win the 2016 World Series.

Can this season be considered successful if the Cubs don't win it all? That's been one of the most

common conversations about the team on social media and among on-air talking heads since the Cubs finished "winning the off-season" with their $184 million signing of outfielder Jason Heyward.

"On paper's one thing," another Cubs newcomer, John Lackey, said. "We've got to go out and get it done."

Lackey, who won World Series clinchers for two different teams, knows the fragile nature of baseball expectations as well as anyone in the clubhouse – part of Boston's epic 2011 September collapse and leader in an odds-beating 2013 Boston championship two years later. That's part of why he was signed.

Cubs president Theo Epstein certainly didn't

WORLD SERIES CHAMPIONS

7

set out to win anything during the winter.

"It is an unbelievable dynamic the last few years how the winners of the offseason tend to be miserable the following September," he said even before the team's flurry of moves in December. "I look forward to one day when we might lose the offseason altogether because it'll probably mean that we had so many different options internally to address whatever needs arose during the previous season. We're not in that position yet."

But they are sitting on an enviable lode of talent and potential as pitchers and catcher report in Mesa, Ariz. – one of the biggest national storylines in baseball as they chase their 108-year-old ghost.

The only certainty at this point is how foolish it is to count on expectations to unfold according to plan for 162 games – much less to make the only measure of success a title in a sport almost unique for how many of the best teams often fall short.

Epstein admittedly pooled a lot of resources into this offseason to take advantage of both the deeper markets of available players as well as what looks like an especially strong window of immediate opportunity for the Cubs.

But he also is the first to admit the tenuous nature of best-laid plans in his business.

"Our goal all along is to win the World Series," Epstein said when asked about what seems like an accelerated timeline for a title. "But you have to prioritize shorter-term goals in order to get there.

"The first goal is just to come together as a team and grind through the season, knowing there's going to be a lot of adversity along the way, knowing we have to connect as a unit in order to play well and persevere."

"Then you want to make sure you get into October, and the best way to do that by far is to win your division," Epstein said. "So like last year our goal is to win the division. And there's no doubt every player who had to watch the Mets celebrate on the field is extraordinarily hungry to win eight more games in October than we did last year.

"We're unified by that common goal," he said. "It's the most important thing in the lives of a lot of people – fans, players, front office alike. And we're out to reach our goals this year and make a lot of people happy, knowing that there's going to be a lot of ups and downs along the way." ■

WORLD SERIES CHAMPIONS

Cubs starting pitcher Jake Arrieta takes the mound during opening night. *AP Photo*

Regular Season

CHICAGO CUBS 9 • LOS ANGELES ANGELS 0

Will The Cubs Ever Lose? It's Within The Realm of Possibility

Cubs catcher Miguel Montero drills a sixth-inning home run. *AP Photo*

by RICK MORRISSEY

Is this how the 161 other victories are going to go?

Wait, what? It's not going to be this easy for the Cubs? There could be actual struggles ahead? Maybe even an occasional dark cloud, baseball-wise?

If you say so. But with expectations sky-high coming into the Cubs' opener followed by their 9-0 domination of the Angels on Monday night, you can understand how a person might think the World Series will go to the first undefeated team in major-league history.

You're right, of course. Better to take a conservative view of things. I can easily see the

WORLD SERIES CHAMPIONS

Cubs losing to the Mets on June 30. I think.

OK, enough. The Cubs looked like a team willing and able to carry the favorites role this season.

But it was one game. Let's not lather up the true believers out there any more than they already are. They're giving each other sponge baths on Twitter as we speak.

Catcher Miguel Montero is not going to go 2-for-5 with a home run and three runs batted in every game.

Leadoff hitter Dexter Fowler is not going to have three hits and a walk every game.

Jake Arrieta can't pitch every game of the season, although somebody show me the science that says he can't. OK, Arrieta can't allow just two hits over seven innings every game, as he did Monday. At least, I don't think so.

Opening Day couldn't have gone any better for the Cubs. Fowler started the game with a double, and two batters later, Anthony Rizzo drove him in. Jorge Soler, a guy the Cubs want to find at-bats for, singled in a run in the fourth. Matt Szczur had a three-run double in the ninth. We all saw that coming.

"It was really a fun game to manage," Cubs skipper Joe Maddon said. "We had to do absolutely nothing (as a coaching staff). It was great."

Nobody forgot how good Arrieta is, but it was nice of him to remind us anyway. After five innings, he had thrown 58 pitches and Angels ace Garrett Richards had thrown 97.

Arrieta has not come down to earth since last year's Cy Young season. He is still somewhere above everyone else, floating, stretching, flexing and doing all the things he does to stay above the competition. On Monday, he made the Angels look like kids stuck on a math problem.

Before the game, Maddon had warned everyone not to expect Arrieta to have the same season he had in 2015, when he finished 22-6 with a 1.77 earned-run average. Arrieta does.

"Numbers-wise, it's tough to expect that, but I still do," he said. "I expect to pitch this way every time I take the mound. If I execute, I pound the strike zone with my stuff and keep 'em guessing, I have a pretty good opportunity to have a good year."

There was a sizable contingent of Cubs fans at Angel Stadium, and their "Let's Go, Cub-bies" chant will find its way into many a ballpark this season. There are lots of Cubs fans nationwide,

and there will be plenty of reasons to cheer.

If you're looking for reasons to worry, it was hard to find any after Game 1. Almost everyone did something positive.

Afterward, Arrieta waited to congratulate his

teammates outside the clubhouse. There was lots of high-fives and back-slapping. You wouldn't have thought it was the first game of the season. But when your last game was a loss in the National League Championship Series six months ago, a celebration is allowed.

"Now we need to carry this over to tomorrow," Arrieta said. "We set the tone pretty nicely for ourselves."

Warning: You can't win them all. Reportedly.■

WORLD SERIES CHAMPIONS

Cubs President of Baseball Operations Theo Epstein

Inset: Epstein and Cubs manager Joe Maddon share a laugh during batting practice. *AP Photos*

Cubs Are A Lot More Than "Some Geeky Stat Team"

by RICK MORRISSEY

If Theo Epstein lived in a city populated solely by stats enthusiasts, he'd never have to buy his own drink. But the Cubs president of baseball operations bristles at the idea that the franchise's recent success is due to some combination of algorithm and artificial intelligence.

"As an organization, if you had to classify where our advantages are these days, if we have any relative to the other teams, I think it's more on the humanist side than it is on the analytical side," he said. "Every organization is doing analytics now. Maybe there's a few breakthroughs here and there still to come, but everyone is doing the same stuff.

"I think one of the things that we do well that gives us a bit of an edge relative to some organizations is we understand the game is played by human beings, and we really encourage guys to be themselves and let their true talent come out.

"It's ironic because I think we are probably painted with a brush as if we're some geeky stat team. That's fine, too. There's a lot of great work that our guys do in that area. But there's no doubt there is a really welcoming environment. It's a humanistic approach to player development, to team building, to showing up for work every day."

There's a certain self-help-book feel to all this talk of culture and team building, and a lot of it comes from Cubs manager Joe Maddon. But Epstein says that whatever comes out of Maddon's mouth is connected to his heart, that beating organ not beholden to numbers or equations.

"He's the real leader of what we're doing here, the culture part I'm talking about, where we let guys be themselves, allow young players to feel comfortable and adjust quickly," he said. "I don't think suits can really pull that off throwing out ideas from the front office. That's a hard thing to pull off in the clubhouse and on the field. Joe coming in really was that last piece of the puzzle for our culture."

In that culture, there is no dress code. In that culture, against what most people would consider reason, the club has held tight to catcher David Ross, who batted .176 last season. Maddon believes Ross is so good for team unity that he doesn't care how bad he is at the plate. Ross'

teammates rave about his ability to connect with different personalities. He's flesh and blood, just like Jake Arrieta is, just like Kris Bryant is.

Those very human players helped the Cubs win 97 regular-season games last season and advance to the National League Championship Series. But it's worth noting that the Cubs finished behind the Cardinals and the Pirates in the NL Central last season. And Epstein very much wants to note it.

"We try to walk around here and remind ourselves that we are a defending third-place team," he said. "We're at an interesting juncture because it's obvious the opportunity that lies before us and how much talent and how much character there is in our clubhouse. But we haven't accomplished anything yet - truly. It's not just a line. We haven't. We have to go out and do it. We have to come together. We have to overcome the adversity. We're excited about it."

If anybody needs a reminder about not getting overconfident, it would be those Cubs fans who think a World Series title in the near future is preordained. Somewhere along the way, tired, hunched-over shuffles have given way to struts. It's an amazing phenomenon considering the Cubs haven't won a championship since 1908.

"I understand the tendency of folks to get ahead of themselves a little bit," Epstein said. "It is a bit of a boomerang effect, where you've been on the other side for so long that you can't find that happy middle ground of cautious optimism or understanding all the things that we hope go right but could go wrong. I understand that.

"But the 25 players in the clubhouse and the greater organization, they're pretty immune to that. They're not going to get wrapped up in any overly optimistic thinking or complacency. There really is a great vibe – good people brought together for a noble cause feeling connected with each other and ready to go work for it. What more could you ask for this time of year?" ∎

Cubs starting pitcher Jake Arrieta, right, celebrates with catcher David Ross after the final out of his no-hitter. *AP Photo*

CHICAGO CUBS 16   •   CINCINNATI REDS 0

Arrieta Throws Second No-Hitter As Cubs Beat Reds

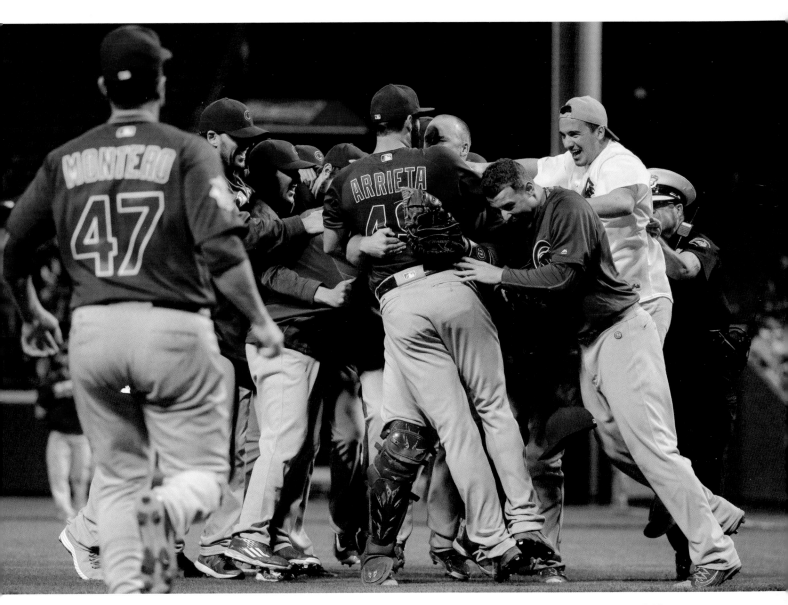

A fan who ran onto the field celebrates the no-hitter with Cubs starting pitcher Jake Arrieta and teammates. *AP Photo*

by GORDON WITTENMYER

After Jake Arrieta's second start of the season, a writer joked that if he kept it up, he might win 30 of his 33 starts this year.

"Why not 33?" Arrieta said flatly, leaving just enough room to doubt whether he was kidding.

Then he goes out on a soggy night in Cincinnati and does what he did Thursday – throwing a second no-hitter in 11 regular-season starts – and you start to wonder just how far-fetched any of it is.

The National League's reigning Cy Young winner struggled with command in the early innings

WORLD SERIES CHAMPIONS

but finished stronger than he started to dominate the Reds during a 16-0 victory at Great American Ballpark and become the first pitcher in franchise history with no-hitters in consecutive seasons.

"That's why he won the Cy Young last year. He's got the capability of doing that every night out," said catcher David Ross, who had a key pickoff after a fourth-inning walk. "I think mentally he expects to do that. He's not shocked when he does stuff like that."

Arrieta, who no-hit the Dodgers in Los Angeles eight months ago, is the third Cubs pitcher with multiple no-hitters, the first since Ken Holtzman had two in the 1970s. The other, Larry Corcoran,

results, you can play a big part in the way certain things unfold. That's why I feel like I have a good chance to win every time I take the mound."

The right-hander walked four but faced only two over the minimum, thanks to Ross's pickoff and a 6-4-3 double play to end the sixth. He struck out six.

Despite a pitch count at 85 through six innings, manager Joe Maddon said he had no intention of pulling Arrieta from the game with the no-hitter intact at any point – a policy set during spring training.

"You never want to interfere with somebody's greatness," Maddon said. "And that's really special for him and for the organization to have another no-hitter being thrown. As a manager you try to stay out of the way of those moments."

Arrieta made it easy by needing just nine pitches each for the seventh and eighth innings.

"It feels different the second time," Arrieta said. "I was a little more relaxed as the game progressed."

What's next? He already set major-league records with his final two months (0.41 ERA), his second half (0.75) and final 20 starts (0.86) of last season.

Add this year's four-game start to his season, and over his last 24 regular-season starts, he's 20-1 with a 0.86 ERA (178 innings).

Over his last 16: 15-0 with a 0.53 ERA (119 1/3 innings).

"It didn't even look like he had his best stuff today, and he goes out there and throws a no-hitter," said third baseman Kris Bryant, who made several key defensive plays and added two homers and six RBIs to the scoring. "He's just the best pitcher I've seen."

"What can I say, man?" said Maddon. "I mean, he was spectacular." ■

had three in the 1880s.

"Part of every pitcher's mental makeup at this level is you have to expect certain things out of yourself," said Arrieta, whose Pilates and yoga regimens are the stuff of clubhouse legend. "The preparation is what allows the success to happen naturally, and even though you can't dictate the

Willson Contreras hits a two-run home run during his first big league at-bat.
AP Photo

JUNE 19, 2016   WRIGLEY FIELD   CHICAGO, ILLINOIS

CHICAGO CUBS 10   •   PITTSBURGH PIRATES 5

Hendricks Strikes Out 12, Cubs Power Through Pirates

Cubs starter Kyle Hendricks struck out 12 in his six-inning stint. *AP Photo*

by JEFF ARNOLD

Sometimes, Joe Maddon preached on Sunday, it's not all about the hits.

Oh, the Cubs have had plenty this season when they entered Father's Day with a double-digit advantage in the standings over those chasing them in the National League's Central Division. But in a season when hardly anything has sidetracked the Cubs, the starting pitching has admirably helped carry the load.

On Sunday night, Kyle Hendricks picked up where Jake Arrieta and Jon Lester left off before him. Hendricks helped complete a weekend sweep of the Pirates with a nationally-televised 10-5 victory in front of 41,024 at Wrigley Field as the Cubs moved to 47-20 on the season.

Hendricks struck out a career-high 12 over six innings and allowed seven hits without issuing a walk.

Of course, the Cubs' offense provided him plenty to work with.

The Cubs, who slugged five home runs – including a two-run shot by prized rookie catcher Willson Contreras – wasted no time in getting to Pirates' starter Jameson Taillon, who carried a no-hitter into the seventh inning of his previous start. Anthony Rizzo's RBI single in the first inning got the Cubs rolling before Maddon's productive lineup clicked into power mode for the second straight night.

After slugging three home runs in Saturday night's 4-3 victory, Javier Baez, Kris Bryant and Rizzo connected off of Taillon (1-1) to extend the lead to 4-0 after three innings. Bryant and Rizzo, who each hit their 17th homers of the season on back-to-back solo shots in the third inning to give Hendricks a comfortable cushion to work with.

Contreras extended the Cubs' lead to 6-1 in the sixth inning when he drove a two-run home run into the center field bleachers on the first pitch he saw. Contreras, who was called up from Class AAA Iowa on Friday, received a standing ovation when he walked to the plate Sunday night.

One pitch and his first big-league homer later, Contreras made a curtain-call appearance at the top of the dugout steps after connecting on the Cubs' fourth home run of the night.

Meanwhile, Hendricks (5-6) cruised through 3 2/3 innings and struck out nine of the first 14 hitters he faced. Josh Harrison broke up the shutout with two outs in the fourth with a solo home run. From there, Hendricks allowed only two hits over his final two innings, flummoxing the Pirates, who have now dropped five straight games and 10 of their last 11.

Pittsburgh trimmed the deficit to 6-4 in the seventh inning on Starling Marte's two-run triple off of reliever Adam Warren, who also gave up a RBI infield single to Jung Ho Kang. Both runs were charged to Clayton Richard, who gave up a single and walk before Warren surrendered the triple to Marte. The Pirates added a run in the ninth on an Andrew McCutchen RBI single.

But just when the Pirates made things interesting, the Cubs' offense piled more on.

Addison Russell's two-run homer capped a four-run eighth inning, which also included a Rizzo RBI single and a Ben Zobrist run-scoring fielder's choice that scored Bryant, who beat the tag at the plate.■

Addison Russell, right, celebrates with Anthony Rizzo after hitting a two-run home run during the seventh inning. *AP Photo*

Young Veteran Rizzo Sets Tone

by GORDON WITTENMYER

As the Cubs open their first World Series in 71 years, the left-handed power-hitting star of this big stage is Anthony Rizzo.

The first cornerstone locked into place during Theo Epstein's organizational rebuilding effort, Rizzo is just four years removed from a 101-loss season, three weeks removed from closing out a 103-win season – and four wins away from doing what only Frank Chance has done as a Cubs first baseman.

"It was definitely a process, but it was a process that sure benefitted me, in a bigger way than a lot of these guys," Rizzo said of the five-season rise toward the World Series opener in Cleveland against Indians ace Corey Kluber.

"I give [the front office] a lot of credit, and everything they've done to this point is huge."

The trade for Rizzo in January 2012 certainly has proved to be huge, if not predictable. The original Red Sox draftee under Epstein and Jed Hoyer already had been traded from Epstein to Hoyer after Hoyer took over as general manager in San Diego, before eventually being acquired for the third time by Hoyer when the front office team moved to Chicago.

Now he's the 27-year-old MVP-candidate veteran on a team of early-20-somethings. The fact he might be more of a kid than any of them is a big part of the influence teammates say has helped this team get so far.

"His personality is what this team's all about really," said World Series veteran catcher David Ross. "Just being able to embrace the moment and still have fun says a lot about him."

Rizzo kissed his bat for a national magazine cover. He kissed the baseball from the last out of Saturday night's pennant clincher against the Dodgers. And then he said he was going to sleep with the ball that night.

"The ball stayed in my car overnight because I couldn't drive home [Saturday]," he said. "I was really nervous about that. The ball's safe now."

The guy who routinely stops at locker stalls in all corners of the clubhouse for chats with teammates before games decided in Los Angeles to take a bat belonging to Matt Szczur – who wasn't even on the playoff roster – and turned Szczur into a celebrity by hitting a home run in a Game 4 Cubs win. He's 7-for-12 since then –

Rizzo, right, and David Ross celebrate their division title.
AP Photo

and now goes from the lefty-heavy Dodgers to the right-leaning Indians pitching staff.

"I just hope he uses the same bat," teammate Jake Arrieta said.

He and second baseman Javy Baez have turned into the NL's version of Elvis Andrus and Adrian Beltre on infield popups twice in the last two games, with Baez cutting in front of Rizzo to try to steal the catch – Rizzo playfully tossing the ball into Baez's chest after the first one.

"We just have fun," Rizzo said. "It's a way of slowing the game down, especially on popups. I know he can handle it, and he knows I can handle it."

Said Arrieta: "To see those guys be able to do that kind of a thing in such a big game means a lot. They're not uptight. These guys are still having fun even though it's the biggest game of their career."

What looks especially big is Rizzo's potential impact on a series in which he'll bat third against a team whose only real threat for trying to neutralize him from the left side is reliever Andrew Miller.

"Righty, lefty, ambidextrous, whatever they are, we've got to be ready to face them," Rizzo said. "As long as we get the wins, it's not individual now." ∎

Chicago Cubs National League All Stars, Ben Zobrist (18), from left, Addison Russell (27), Dexter Fowler (24), Kris Bryant (17), Jake Arrieta (49), Jon Lester (34) and Anthony Rizzo (44) pose for a photo with their All Star jerseys. *AP Photo*

Cubs catcher Miguel Montero, left, and relief pitcher Aroldis Chapman celebrate the Cubs' 8-1 win over the Chicago White Sox. *AP Photo*

Cubs Rout Sox As Chapman Makes Triple-Digit Cub Debut

Cubs relief pitcher Aroldis Chapman delivers in this multiple exposure photo during the ninth inning. *AP Photo*

by GORDON WITTENMYER

The Cubs' big eighth inning turned Wednesday night's victory into an 8-1 rout, but that didn't seem to diminish the drama surrounding the debut of controversial closer Aroldis Chapman as he entered to pitch the ninth inning against the White Sox at Wrigley Field.

A smattering of boos could be heard amid a much louder chorus of cheers. And the boos turned to oohs (and aahs) when his first pitch registered a 101 reading on the scoreboard radar display.

Second pitch: 101. Third pitch: 102.

By the time pinch-hitter Avisail Garcia struck out looking at a 103 mph fastball to end the game, Cubs history had come full circle, from Three Finger Brown to Three Digit Chapman – with the

WORLD SERIES CHAMPIONS

same World Series expectations attached.

"It's just entertaining to watch the gun, beyond everything else," Cubs manager Joe Maddon said. "Of course, you're looking to get the win, but it's different, man. He's a different kind of pitcher. You don't see that [but] every 100 years or so."

Chapman got off to a rocky start with Chicago media Tuesday over a series of non-answers to questions about his domestic-violence suspension this year, and on Wednesday initially refused to talk with media after the game, visibly upset.

Eventually, with the help of some bridge building by catcher Miguel Montero, Chapman took a few questions.

"The adrenaline was pretty good even though it wasn't a save situation," Chapman said, with Montero translating from Spanish. "It was fun to hear the crowd cheering for me."

Chapman, pitching for the first time since Saturday, was in line for the save until the Cubs scored five in the eighth, capped by 22-year-old Addison Russell's first career grand slam, the Cubs' third homer of the game (also Kris Bryant and Javy Baez).

Russell is the youngest Cub to hit a grand slam since 1962 (Nelson Mathews, 20).

"It was almost good that it wasn't a save situation," Maddon said, "just to allow him to get his feet on the ground. There were a lot of positives out of that moment right there.

"I give the guy some credit for going out there in somewhat of a difficult situation based on the last couple days," Maddon added. "I don't even know how much rest he's gotten."

As for the promise of triple-digit ninth innings the rest of the season?

"It was very cool," Maddon said. "I've seen it on the wrong side. It's nice to have it on your side."

For almost six innings it was the White Sox debut of Anthony Ranaudo that provided much of the drama.

All Cubs Maddon knew about Ranaudo before the game was what the manager saw on some video from a minor-league game.

"I saw some pitches up," Maddon said.

A few hours later, so did Bryant and Baez.

Bryant's solo homer with one out in the sixth not only tied the game, but also broke up Ranaudo's no-hit bit.

Until then, the right-hander also accounted for the game's only run, with a homer off Jason Hammel leading off the fifth. It was the first career hit for Ranaudo, 26.

Hammel (10-5) pitched seven strong innings to win his third straight start out of the All-Star break, tying his career high in wins for a season.

He struck out seven, walked two and pitched out of a two-on, one-out jam in the fourth by getting former Cub Dioner Navarro to fly to center and striking out Monday night's hero Tyler Saladino.

"He was outstanding," Maddon said.■

Cubs third baseman Kris Bryant connects on a home run off Chicago White Sox pitcher Anthony Ranaudo. *AP Photo*

Anthony Rizzo gets a high-five after his walk drove in the game-winning RBI in the 10th inning. *AP Photo*

CHICAGO CUBS 4   •   ST. LOUIS CARDINALS 3

Cubs Walk Off, Literally, For 10th Straight Win

Catcher David Ross tags out the Cardinals Matt Carpenter on a play at home plate. *AP Photo*

—— by **GORDON WITTENMYER** ——

Just when it looked like the drama this season was over for the Cubs, along came the Cardinals.

And 12 innings later, the Cubs had their third walkoff victory in their last seven home games, their 10th victory in a row overall and their 13th in 14 games.

The 4-3 victory – on Anthony Rizzo's two-out bases-loaded walk against Zach Duke – boosted the biggest division lead in baseball to a season-high 13 games.

Over?

Don't try to tell the Cubs there's no drama left in this season.

"Especially against the Cardinals," Rizzo said. "Emotions are a little higher. We battle. That's kind of our identity."

Until this walkoff-fueled winning streak, the

WORLD SERIES CHAMPIONS

33

Cubs had one walkoff all year. These days they don't even have to swing the bat to get one.

"We have a walkoff walk, a walkoff wild pitch [Aug. 3], and one on a bunt by a pitcher [July 31]," Rizzo said. "It's going our way. We've just got to keep it going."

How do they keep pulling these off?

"I guess just put Lack in the bullpen at the end," said starter Jon Lester of John Lackey, the starting pitcher who was warming up in the 11th just before the game-winner scored - 12 days after he was doing the same thing when that game-winner scored in the 12th.

The Cubs fell behind 2-0, came back to take the lead with a three-run sixth, then watched pinch-hitter Randal Grichuk tie it in the seventh with a homer off Travis Wood.

Then came the drama – which included a big blow to Matt Holliday's right hand and the Cardinals' playoff chances in the 10th, when Mike Montgomery hit the Cards' slugger with a pitch.

X-rays revealed a broken thumb.

"That's awful," manager Joe Maddon said. "He's a very important player on their team."

As for the rivalry, it may not have looked like it had much juice in it going into the game.

"This should bring out the best in everybody – them and us," Maddon said before the opener of a four-game series between the century-long rivals. "If you cant' get up for playing these particular games, then just do something else."

On an 87-degree night, the Cubs and Cards turned up the heat on a game that went from a pitching duel to a late-inning fight.

"There's no animosity. I think it's called respect," Maddon said of the rival emotions. "A lot of respect from us to them, from me to them, based on a tremendous tradition that they've built up."

By the time Chris Coghlan tied the game after calling timeout – only to not get the timeout, then step back in and quickly swing for a two-run single – the drama was back in the rivalry, if not the division race.

The whole scene, all night, at Wrigley was almost enough to make anyone watching forget the Cubs have nearly lapped the National League Central field with seven weeks to play.

"Yeah, I am surprised that there is that kind of a gap," Maddon said. "Absolutely surprised.

"But I'm not taking anything for granted."■

Shortstop Addison Russell strokes his 16th double of the year during the eighth inning. *AP Photo*

Cubs manager Joe Maddon talks to the media before a recent game. ***AP Photo***

Believe It: With Joe Maddon Behind Them, Cubs Think Anything Is Possible

by RICK MORRISSEY

Last season, the Cubs were beyond belief. Lots of people believed the team was going to be good, but not 97 victories good and surely not National League Championship Series good.

"I think we just proved ourselves right," first baseman Anthony Rizzo said. "We never go out trying to prove anyone wrong. It's just a matter of us believing."

The issue of belief is a big one, or at least the Cubs believe it is. If there was one thing manager Joe Maddon was brought in for, it was his ability to make players believe in themselves. He could make a mortician believe he's a big-league shortstop. There's a decent chance he could convince a mortician that death isn't an inevitability.

"He's always going to be positive," said Cubs second baseman Ben Zobrist, who played for the Maddon in Tampa Bay. "He's always going to say we're going to do it and believe it - but he really does believe that. You have to believe that you are a playoff team.

"... Sometimes we wait for the action to happen first, and then we believe. He's all about the opposite of that: 'No, you've got to believe and we'll see it happen.' I do understand the importance of execution, and he does too. We all understand at this level that you've got to execute. But if you don't believe it first, then you're going to have a lot harder time actually executing the way you're capable of."

In 2011, the Rays started the season 0-6. At that point, Maddon convened a meeting and informed the players that they would make the postseason, Zobrist said. And they did as a wild-card team, despite trailing Boston by nine games in September.

"Some of us rolled our eyes," Zobrist said of the meeting. "You have a hard time believing it at that moment, but Joe believed it. The true mettle of our team showed the rest of that month. We ended up playing really well."

If the manager always believes, can his belief be trusted? It's the converse of the Boy Who Cried Wolf. If Maddon is always upbeat, if his message is always that the team is this close to whatever the goal is, will players eventually stop listening to him? It happened with a few of his players in Tampa Bay.

In the first week of Cubs camp this winter, Maddon advanced at least two themes for the season – "embrace the target" and "the process is the anchor." T-shirt makers are scrambling as we speak.

Do some players listen to Maddon's slogans and say, "Enough?"

"Of course," Zobrist said. "Who doesn't do that with their boss? But at the same time, it's his job to lead us in the direction he feels we need to go. We don't have to necessarily agree with everything that he says or does, but we're all aimed at the same purpose.

"He's definitely a unique leader in that respect. He does it his way, and he doesn't care. You can either follow along or not, but his job is to lead the best way he knows how. That's what we see, his authenticity. The most important thing is authenticity and genuine personality. He really cares. He really wants to win."

The Cubs are coming off one of their best seasons in decades, so all of this might seem like a moot discussion. They seem destined for another great year. There is a glut of belief. But there will be difficulties this season because there almost always are difficulties in a season. Injuries. Slumping players. Friction between teammates.

The Cubs spend a lot of time talking about their culture, which they say is based on being yourself and caring for your teammates. That, they believe, will lead to winning, which is the ultimate goal.■

Albert Almora Jr., right, celebrates with Chris Coghlan after hitting a two-run home run during the fifth inning. *AP Photo*

SEPTEMBER 16, 2016   WRIGLEY FIELD   CHICAGO, ILLINOIS

CHICAGO CUBS 5   •   MILWAUKEE BREWERS 4

Cubs Celebrate –
But Keep Their Eye On The Prize

Cubs manager Joe Maddon and Kris Bryant celebrate their division title after defeating the Milwaukee Brewers.   *AP Photo*

by MARK POTASH

With the music turned up full blast, the lights turned down low and the beer spraying, the champagne flowing and owner Tom Ricketts doing shots, the Cubs clubhouse turned into a night club gone haywire in a celebration that was both a long time coming and yet - the Cubs hope – just the first step toward Chicago baseball immortality.

The Cubs celebrated like they hadn't won a division title in 108 years. But they earned the right with one of the most dominant seasons a Chicago baseball team has ever had – clinching the National League Central Division title with 16 games to go.

"We just won one of the toughest divisions in all of baseball and we did it by a landslide," first baseman Anthony Rizzo said. "We have to

WORLD SERIES CHAMPIONS

celebrate this because we've been so good all year. This is a huge steppingstone to where we want to be and we're going to celebrate every stop along the way."

And at the same time, the Cubs were steadfast about keeping the big picture in focus. This team expects to win the World Series.

"There's much more left for the team," pitcher Kyle Hendricks said. "This is only the first baby step. We know where we want to go and it's a lot more than just the division."

A year ago, the Cubs finished third in the Central and made the playoffs as the second wild-card team. This group basked in the satisfaction of raising the bar themselves and exceeding it. You don't have to win your division to win the World Series. But this team took a huge step by winning the Central this season.

"This is what we preached in spring training is win the division," Rizzo said. "We put ourselves in position to line ourselves up with how we want to attack the playoffs [and] whoever we play. So enjoy it, let it sink in for a few days and get ready for October."

After clinching the division when the Giants beat the Cardinals on the West Coast on Thursday night, the Cubs (94-53) were going to celebrate whether they won or lost Friday against the Milwaukee Brewers. But in typical fashion, they found a way to make the moment special, with a thrilling 5-4 victory on Miguel Montero's walk-off homer leading off the 10th inning.

With a make-shift lineup that did not include Rizzo, Kris Bryant, Addison Russell, Ben Zobrist, Dexter Fowler or Jason Heyward, the Cubs trailed 4-2 in the ninth, but rallied behind Willson Contreras, Chris Coghlan and Addison Russell to tie the game in the ninth. It was only a matter of time after that, and Montero ended it quickly, setting an appropriate mood for the raucous

celebration that followed.

"The perfect way – a walk-off win and we come in here to celebrate. It doesn't get any better than that," Bryant said. "This team has so much resilience. We're never going to give up. You saw that in the game today. I haven't had this much fun playing baseball in a long time."

Just three more celebrations to go. There's no doubt this team has enough gas in the tank for that.

"We could get used to [these celebrations]," Hendricks said. "We've definitely got the right guys to lead us."■

WORLD SERIES CHAMPIONS

Starting pitcher Kyle Hendricks lowered his league-leading ERA to 1.99 with six scoreless innings. *AP Photo*

Hendricks Beats Bucs For Cubs' 100th Win

Cubs third baseman Javier Baez hits a grand slam during the fourth inning. He finished the day with six run batted in. *AP Photo*

by GORDON WITTENMYER

Don't try to tell Kyle Hendricks and the rest of the Cubs that this final week of regular season games doesn't mean anything.

In the opener of a four-game series at PNC Park on Monday night, they looked as relentless as the Pirateslooked feckless in a 12-2 Cubs victory that gave the Cubs 100 wins in a season for the first time in 71 years – and put Hendricks on the brink of his own place in franchise history.

With Javy Baez leading the way on the big scoring night with six RBIs – including a grand slam – Hendricks did the rest with six scoreless innings to lower his major-league-leading ERA to 1.99 with one start left.

The poster boy for one-start-at-a-time focus this season, even Hendricks admits he can allow for a thought or two about becoming the first Cub to win an ERA title since Ray Prim in 1945.

"It's really only me or Jon," he said of

WORLD SERIES CHAMPIONS

43

teammate Jon Lester, whose 2.28 ERA ranks second in the majors to Hendricks'. "That's the cool part about it. It's going to go to one of us, and that's awesome."

Hendricks, who said he started to lose command of his sinker as his start progressed Monday, nonetheless didn't issue a walk and pitched out of jams in the third and sixth.

He has been as big a reason for the Cubs' sixth 100-win season in franchise history as anybody on the roster.

"Kyle doing what he's doing, obviously, we did not anticipate all of this," manager Joe Maddon said of the right-hander, who opened the season as the Cubs' fifth starter and will finish as their Game 2 playoff starter.

"It's been a big difference for us that he's been able to do what he's done this year, no question," Maddon said.

Hendricks' 1.99 ERA would rank second only to teammate Jake Arrieta's 1.77 last year among Cubs pitchers since 1950.

"He's been unbelievable," said veteran Travis Wood, an all-star starter three years ago and key

"By no means is this a fluke," Maddon said. "This is something that can carry on for years. It's not an anomaly. This is how good he's capable of being"

Anomaly? Hendricks, 26, improved to 31-17 with a 2.87 ERA in 74 career starts (plus a scoreless two-inning relief outing this year).

"One of my goals coming into the year was just to kind of establish who I was, that I could get guys out on a consistent basis," he said, "and gain the feel for all these different kinds of hitters. So when I got through the end of the year here with some of the success I saw, it definitely helped a lot looking toward the future and what I can do.

"It's been a big year for me just learning, and to see those results."

Making History

With one start remaining, Kyle Hendricks is in position to win the Cubs' first National League ERA title in 71 years. Hendricks listed with the franchise's ERA champions (*-denotes led/leads both AL and NL):

ERA CHAMPIONS

Year	Player	ERA
2016	Kyle Hendricks	1.99*
1945	Ray Prim	2.40
1938	Bill Lee	2.66*
1932	Lon Warneke	2.37*
1920	Grover Alexander	1.91*
1919	Grover Alexander	1.72
1918	Hippo Vaughn	1.74
1910	King Cole	1.80
1907	Jack Pfiester	1.15*
1906	Three Finger Brown	1.04*
1902	Jack Taylor	1.29*
1898	Clark Griffith	1.88
1882	Larry Corcoran	1.95

Note: Brown's mark in 1906 is the franchise record.

Chicago Fire
If the season ended today, Kyle Hendricks' and Jon Lester's 2016 ERAs would rank among the Cubs' top five since 1950:

Player, Year	ERA
Jake Arrieta, 2015	1.77
Kyle Hendricks, 2016	1.99
Dick Ellsworth, 1963	2.11
Greg Maddux, 1992	2.18
Jon Lester, 2016	2.28
Mark Prior, 2003	2.43
Bill Hands, 1969	2.49
Mike Morgan, 1992	2.55
Larry Jackson, 1963	2.55
Warren Hacker, 1952	2.58
Fergie Jenkins, 1968	2.63

member of the Cubs' bullpen. "He knows how to manipulate the balls in ways a lot of pitchers don't, keeps people off balance."

"He just finds a way to get them to make weak contact," said MVP candidate Kris Bryant, who hit his 39th homer and passed the 100-RBI mark (101) Monday. "It's unbelievable what he can do."

Hendricks' run dates back to a pair of scoreless performances in his final two starts of last season and accelerated this year when he added an improved curve ball and more liberal use of a four-seam fastball to the best changeup on the staff.

WORLD SERIES CHAMPIONS

2016 Cubs vs. 2015 Cubs, Best Of Seven? Not Even Close

by STEVE GREENBERG

Remember the 2015 Cubs? Boy, what a bunch of bums they were.

Just ask them.

"I certainly think this team is a whole lot better," second-year star Kris Bryant said before game against the Pirates.

Last year's Cubs were the hottest team in baseball down the stretch, with the good times rolling all the way through to the NLCS. True, if you look at each team through Sept. 27 of its respective season, the 2016 Cubs are 10 games better in the won-loss department. But what if this year's team and last year's team met in a space-time-continuum-defying seven-game series?

Wouldn't it at least be a fair fight?

"We would crush that team," Bryant said.

Guess that's a no.

Actually, there are those who aren't as quick to dismiss a hard-charging bunch that won 45 of 63 games to close the regular season and had the temerity to wipe the higher-seeded Pirates and Cardinals out of the playoffs.

"I think it would go seven games," catcher Miguel Montero said. "Obviously, this is a better team, but it's not all about that. Last year's team was special, too. We came to play like we do this year."

Reliever Travis Wood, who has been with the Cubs longer than any of his teammates, concurred with Montero.

Sort of.

"There'd be a battle, I think. We were a great team last year," he said. "Although, we definitely have improved."

At what, exactly?

"I guess at everything."

Gee, is that all?

According to Bryant, all you have to do is "just look up and down" at the roster to see a vastly improved version of what the Cubs were in 2015.

He's probably right about that. The additions of big-time veterans Jason Heyward, John Lackey and Aroldis Chapman clearly took the team's talent to a different level. Bryant has progressed from N.L. Rookie of the Year to leading MVP candidate. Shortstop Addison Russell is much more dynamic in Year 2 than he was as a rookie. First baseman Anthony Rizzo is better than ever.

Then there's the Cubs' ridiculously good defense, which at times this season has been the talk of baseball.

Man, where does it stop?

"The list of improvements? It just goes on and on and on," Russell said. "All facets of the game have been improved. And it's not just the talent we have or the individual improvements guys have made. We're also improved mentally. We were good last year, but I don't really think it's close between the two teams."

Infielder Javy Baez maintains that the single biggest difference between the teams is an above-the-neck matter.

"Last year, we worked so hard to get to the playoffs, but then it was like it didn't really matter if we made it to the World Series," he said. "This year, we [have qualified for] the playoffs, but to us it feels like the beginning. The only thing that matters is the World Series."

Oh, and for those of you scoring at home: Baez believes the 2016 Cubs would sweep their 2015 selves.

Manager Joe Maddon has a soft spot for his first Cubs team, which was said by many to have arrived a year ahead of schedule. Maddon describes the fact the team squeezed 97 victories out of the regular season as "kind of crazy, actually."

So let's turn the question around and ask it a different way: Is there anything – anything at all – the 2015 Cubs were better at than the 2016 Cubs?

"I don't think so," Maddon said after roughly a three-second pause in which he appeared to give the matter serious thought.

More likely, he was just being diplomatic. ∎

The addition of big-time veterans John Lackey, Aroldis Chapman and Jason Heyward has increased the Cubs talent level over the 2015 team. *AP Photo*

Cubs starting pitcher Jon Lester runs towards first base after fielding a grounder hit by Giants catcher Buster Posey in the sixth inning. *AP Photo*

Cubs Start Countdown With 1-0 Win Over Giants

Cubs shortstop Addison Russell applies the tag to Giants centerfielder Gorkys Hernandez who was attempting to steal second base during first inning action. *AP Photo*

by GORDON WITTENMYER

One game. One run. One victory for the Cubs.

"So 10 more wins," Kris Bryant said.

Even as they opened the playoffs with a tense, taut game decided on a homer in the bottom of the eighth Friday night at Wrigley Field, the Cubs kept their gaze fixed firmly on the postseason horizon.

"I had a big hit today," said Javy Baez, whose one-out basket shot to left in the eighth off Johnny Cueto lifted Jon Lester and the Cubs to a 1-0 victory over the Giants.

"But we've got to win 10 more games."

Certainly the Cubs enjoyed the moment, not only with their regular post-win party-room event, but also with a bat flip from Baez after launching the high fly ball that left fielder Angel Pagan was camped underneath until the basket caught it instead.

"I thought I hit it really good. I thought it

WORLD SERIES CHAMPIONS

was way farther than that," said Baez of the ball into a 10-mph headwind. "It barely went out, but I still will take it. I didn't mean to show anybody up. But it was a big hit for us."

Lester outdueled Cueto for eight innings in the opener of a series that for at least one night delivered on its promise of dominant starting pitching and low-scoring games.

He put the leadoff man on in the first three innings and pitched out of a second-and-third, two-out jam in the fourth. But he retired the final 13 he faced.

Cueto retired the first 10 he faced and allowed three hits in the eight-inning complete game.

"That's classic playoff baseball in the National League right there," said catcher David Ross – who helped set a defensive tone in the first by throwing out Gorkys Hernandez trying to steal after he'd led off the game with a bunt single. "There was going to be good pitching; we knew that coming in. That's a really good team.

"We know they're good, and we've got a lot of work left to do."

This one didn't get a lot easier even after the home run, especially after closer Aroldis Chapman gave up a two-out double to Buster Posey before

Javier Baez takes a moment to celebrate with Cubs fans after hitting the game-winning home run in the eighth inning. *AP Photo*

BOX SCORE

	1	2	3	4	5	6	7	8	9		R	H	E
San Francisco	0	0	0	0	0	0	0	0	0		0	6	0
Chicago	0	0	0	0	0	0	1	-			1	3	0

Giants	AB	R	H	RBI	BB	SO	AVG.
Hernández CF	4	0	1	0	0	1	.250
Belt 1B	3	0	0	0	0	2	.000
Núñez PH	1	0	0	0	0	0	.000
Posey C	4	0	2	0	0	0	.500
Blanco PR	0	0	0	0	0	0	.000
Pence RF	4	0	1	0	0	0	.250
Pagán LF	3	0	1	0	0	0	.333
Crawford SS	3	0	0	0	0	0	.000
Tomlinson 2B	3	0	0	0	0	1	.000
Gillaspie 3B	3	0	1	0	0	1	.333
Cueto P	3	0	0	0	0	1	.000
Totals	31	0	6	0	0	6	

Cubs	AB	R	H	RBI	BB	SO	AVG.
Fowler CF	3	0	0	0	0	2	.000
Bryant 3B	3	0	1	0	0	1	.333
Rizzo 1B	3	0	0	0	0	0	.000
Zobrist LF	3	0	0	0	0	2	.000
Russell SS	3	0	0	0	0	1	.000
Heyward RF	3	0	0	0	0	0	.000
Báez 2B	3	1	2	1	0	0	.667
Ross C	2	0	0	0	0	1	.000
Coghlan PH	1	0	0	0	0	1	.000
Contreras C	0	0	0	0	0	0	.000
Lester P	2	0	0	0	0	2	.000
La Stella PH	1	0	0	0	0	0	.000
Chapman P	0	0	0	0	0	0	.000
Totals	27	1	3	1	0	10	

Giants	IP	H	R	ER	BB	SO	HR	ERA
Cueto (L, 0-1)	8.0	3	1	1	0	10	1	1.13
Totals	8.0	3	1	1	0	10	1	

Cubs	IP	H	R	ER	BB	SO	HR	ERA
Lester (W, 1-0)	8.0	5	0	0	0	5	0	0.00
Chapman (S, 1)	1.0	1	0	0	0	1	0	0.00
Totals	9.0	6	0	0	0	6	0	

retiring the dangerous Hunter Pence to end the game.

Of course, it's an even-numbered year against the Giants (who won in 2010, 2012 and 2014).

"They've been on that big stage and succeeded," Ross said. "That's a lot of rings in that clubhouse."

But the Cubs had their 103-win success coming into the game, too.

And Lester and Ross have three rings between them.

"Both sides really played an equal kind of a game," Cubs manager Joe Maddon said. "Cueto was outstanding. Jon Lester was outstanding. The defenses played. It was a classic kind of an old-school baseball game."

Classic enough that both teams had run-prevention, defensive lineups in the field – including Giants second-baseman Kelby Tomlinson, who robbed the Cubs of hits twice with diving plays, including an inning-ender in the fourth on Ben Zobrist that saved a run.

And including Baez, the fielding ace who was at second as much for his glove as anything else he might offer from the seventh spot in the order.

"Javy's more than a heavy defensive guy," Ross said. "He's a great defender, but he's a great player." ■

Travis Wood goes deep off of Giants pitcher George Kontos in the fourth inning. Wood became the first relief pitcher since 1924 to hit a postseason home run.
AP Photo

Cubs Take 2-0 Lead To West Coast

Cubs starting pitcher Kyle Hendricks hits a two-run RBI single in the second inning. *AP Photo*

by GORDON WITTENMYER

With all due respect to Madison Bumgarner, who's going to stop these guys?

In Game 2 of the National League Division Series against the ring-jangled Giants, the Cubs had their ERA-champion pitcher get knocked out of the game in the fourth inning by a line drive, their MVP-candidate third baseman make two errors on the same batted ball in the fifth and their Game 1 hero get thrown out at second because he pimped a "home run" that didn't actually get over the fence in the sixth.

And they won.

Saturday's 5-2 victory over ex-Cub Jeff Samardzija and the Giants opened a

WORLD SERIES CHAMPIONS

Cubs second baseman Javier Baez beats the throw home following a single by starting pitcher Kyle Hendricks in the second inning. *AP Photo*

commanding 2-0 series lead in the best-of-five set that heads next to San Francisco.

What could possibly go wrong?

Besides, if Game 2 is any indication, would it matter anyway?

"You got some champs over there, man," Cubs leadoff man Dexter Fowler said. "They've won World Series before. So it's never over."

Come on. Every time the Cubs have ever taken a 2-0 lead in a postseason series – wait a minute. Never mind.

"That's what I'm saying," pitcher and hitter of the night Travis Wood said. "It's baseball. Nothing's ever over. Not until the last out's made. Anything can happen."

The Cubs won the first two games of a

postseason series only twice before in franchise history, the last time in 1984.

"That's crazy," Fowler said.

Not that most of these Cubs have much of a concept of the '80s, much less a few ballgames 32 years ago in San Diego.

"We're too young. I wasn't born in 1984," said Kris Bryant, the presumptive MVP who made those two errors on pinch-hitter Bumgarner's grounder in the fifth – a bobble allowing Bumgarner to reach first, followed by a bad throw allowing him to take second.

"I don't know the history," Bryant added. "We're going to try our best to rewrite our own history."

Again, who's going to stop them?

It was hard to look at the fourth inning Saturday

54

	1	2	3	4	5	6	7	8	9		R	H	E
San Francisco	0	0	2	0	0	0	0	0	0		2	6	1
Chicago	1	3	0	1	0	0	0	-			5	9	3

Giants	AB	R	H	RBI	BB	SO	AVG.
Span CF	4	0	0	0	0	0	.000
Belt 1B	3	0	1	1	0	0	.167
Posey C	4	0	0	0	0	1	.250
Pence RF	4	0	1	0	0	0	.250
Crawford SS	4	0	1	0	0	1	.143
Pagán LF	3	0	1	0	0	0	.333
Gillaspie 3B	2	0	0	0	0	1	.200
Tomlinson PH-3B	2	0	0	0	0	2	.000
Panik 2B	3	1	1	0	0	1	.333
Samardzija P	0	0	0	0	0	0	.000
Blanco PH	1	1	1	1	0	0	1.000
Kontos P	0	0	0	0	0	0	.000
Bumgarner PH	1	0	0	0	0	0	.000
Blach P	0	0	0	0	0	0	.000
Casilla P	0	0	0	0	0	0	.000
Núñez PH	1	0	0	0	0	0	.000
Law P	0	0	0	0	0	0	.000
López P	0	0	0	0	0	0	.000
Strickland P	0	0	0	0	0	0	.000
Totals	32	2	6	2	0	6	

Cubs	AB	R	H	RBI	BB	SO	AVG.
Fowler CF	4	1	1	0	0	1	.143
Bryant 3B	4	0	1	1	0	0	.286
Rizzo 1B	4	0	0	0	0	1	.000
Zobrist LF	4	0	1	1	0	1	.143
Russell SS	4	0	0	0	0	0	.000
Heyward RF	4	1	1	0	0	1	.143
Báez 2B	3	1	1	0	1	2	.500
Contreras C	3	1	2	0	0	0	.667
Hendricks P	1	0	1	2	0	0	1.000
Wood P	1	1	1	1	0	0	1.000
Edwards Jr. P	0	0	0	0	0	0	.000
Montero PH	1	0	0	0	0	0	.000
Montgomery P	0	0	0	0	0	0	.000
Rondón P	0	0	0	0	0	0	.000
Chapman P	0	0	0	0	0	0	.000
Totals	33	5	9	5	1	6	

Giants	IP	H	R	ER	BB	SO	HR	ERA
Samardzija (L, 0-1)	2.0	6	4	4	1	1	0	18.00
Kontos	2.0	1	1	1	0	1	1	4.50
Blach	1.1	0	0	0	2	0	0	0.00
Casilla	0.2	2	0	0	0	0	0	0.00
Law	0.1	0	0	0	0	1	0	0.00
López	0.2	0	0	0	0	0	0	0.00
Strickland	1.0	0	0	0	1	1	0	0.00
Totals	8.0	9	5	5	1	6	1	

Cubs	IP	H	R	ER	BB	SO	HR	ERA
Hendricks	3.2	4	2	2	0	0	0	4.91
Wood (W, 1-0)	1.1	0	0	0	0	2	0	0.00
Edwards Jr. (H, 1)	1.0	1	0	0	0	0	0	0.00
Montgomery (H, 1)	1.1	1	0	0	0	1	0	0.00
Rondón (H, 1)	0.2	0	0	0	0	1	0	0.00
Chapman (S, 2)	1.0	0	0	0	0	2	0	0.00
Totals	9.0	6	2	2	0	6	0	

without at least a fleeting thought about destiny. Or at least depth and ability.

With the Cubs leading 4-2 and two outs in the top of the fourth, Angel Pagan drilled a line drive back to the mound that hit starter Kyle Hendricks on his pitching forearm.

Hendricks, who led major league baseball with a 2.13 ERA, threw a few practice pitches under the supervision of manager Joe Maddon and trainer PJ Mainville, and then was replaced by Wood.

X-rays were negative, and the club said he escaped with a bad bruise.

"Apparently, there's nothing wrong as far as we know right now," Maddon said. "I don't know how long it's going to take for him to be well enough to be able to pitch, but he's fine."

Meanwhile, Wood quickly got the final out of the inning and pitched a scoreless fifth. In between he became only the second relief pitcher in history to hit a postseason homer, first in 92 years (Rosy Ryan of the Giants).

The knockout blow in the series?

"We can't get too big of a head," Wood said. "You've got to stay humble and know that that's a great ballclub over there, because it is."■

San Francisco Giants third baseman Conor Gillaspie drills a two-run triple during the eighth inning. *AP Photo*

Cubs Fall To Giants In Wild 13-Inning Affair

Cubs third baseman Kris Bryant, left, celebrates with third base coach Gary Jones after hitting a game tying two-run home run during the ninth inning. *AP Photo*

by GORDON WITTENMYER

The Cubs did the impossible Monday night. Twice.

And it wasn't good enough in a 6-5, extra-inning loss to the Giants, who staved off elimination at AT&T Park in Game 3 of the National League Division Series.

Brandon Crawford led off the 13th inning with a double to right off taxed reliever Mike Montgomery, and Joe Panik followed with a drive off the right-field wall to drive him home with the game winner.

"That was an incredible game on both sides, and they earned it," said Cubs starter Jake Arrieta, who outpitched all-time postseason ace Madison Bumgarner – and hit a three-run homer off him in the second.

"This is October baseball," Arrieta added. "Obviously, with their pedigree in the playoffs we have our work cut out for us."

"You can never count them out," Cubs shortstop Addison Russell said. "But don't count us out, either."

The Giants' win Monday was their 10th consecutive in the postseason when facing elimination – the longest such streak in baseball history.

WORLD SERIES CHAMPIONS

The Cubs took advantage of one of the best October starting pitchers in history to wear down Bumgarner, whose velocity was down Monday night as his pitch count climbed to 101 through five.

He left the game at that point, the Cubs taking a 3-2 lead into the late innings.

Even after manager Joe Maddon's decision to chance a six-out save from Aroldis Chapman backfired on the Cubs in a three-run Giants' eighth, the Cubs weren't done with the heroics.

That's when MVP favorite Kris Bryant followed Dexter Fowler's leadoff walk in the ninth with a tying, two-run shot to left field off Sergio Romo – Bryant's 40th overall homer this year.

Arrieta's three-run shot in the second seemed to shake the unflappable Bumgarner, who had the bullpen stirring behind him at that point. Did it cross his mind this would be how his season might end?

"No," Bumgarner said. "I don't think anybody was thinking that way. We're hard to put away."

Especially in the eighth inning on this night. That's when White Sox castoff Conor Gillaspie took over.

Less than a week after his home run against Mets closer Jeurys Familia gave the Giants a wild-card victory and put them in this NLDS, his two-run triple off Cubs closer Chapman, just beyond the reach of Albert Almora Jr. in right-center, drove home the tying and go-ahead runs in the bottom of the eighth.

Brandon Crawford followed with a single through the drawn-in Cubs infield for a 5-3 lead.

Chapman, the triple-digit, All-Star closer, was acquired at the trade deadline from the Yankees for moments like this. At least ninth-inning moments like this.

But after Brandon Belt singled off Travis Wood to lead off the eighth, and Buster Posey followed with a walk against Hector Rondon, Maddon went to Chapman for the kind of six-out save Chapman told Maddon this summer he wasn't comfortable with.

And it backfired.

By the time Justin Grimm finished the eighth for Chapman, the Cubs had used four relievers in the inning. And Montgomery took over in the bottom of the ninth, leaving only rookie Carl Edwards Jr. in the bullpen.

"I had it set up before the inning began, based on their lineup construction," said Maddon, who anticipated using Chapman with two outs in the eighth but couldn't get the matchups to play out that way. ∎

Cubs second baseman Javier Baez make an incredible play to throw out the Giants Conor Gillaspie at first base during the sixth inning. *AP Photo*

BOX SCORE

	1	2	3	4	5	6	7	8	9	10	11	12	13	R	H	E
Chicago	0	3	0	0	0	0	0	2	0	0	0	0		5	10	2
San Francisco	0	0	1	0	1	0	0	3	0	0	0	1		6	13	1

Cubs	AB	R	H	RBI	BB	SO	AVG.
Fowler CF	5	1	1	0	1	1	.167
Bryant 3B	5	1	3	2	1	2	.417
Rizzo 1B	6	0	0	0	0	2	.000
Soler LF	3	0	0	0	1	1	.000
Strop P	0	0	0	0	0	0	.000
Wood P	0	0	0	0	0	0	1.000
Rondón P	0	0	0	0	0	0	.000
Almora Jr. RF	2	0	0	0	0	0	.000
Zobrist RF-LF	5	0	1	0	0	0	.167
Montgomery P	0	0	0	0	0	6	.000
Russell SS	5	1	1	0	1	1	.083
Báez 2B	6	1	2	0	0	2	.417
Montero C	3	0	0	0	0	0	.000
Contreras C-LF	2	0	1	0	1	1	.600
Arrieta P	3	1	1	3	0	0	.333
Heyward RF	1	0	0	0	0	1	.125
Chapman P	0	0	0	0	0	0	.000
Grimm P	0	0	0	0	0	0	.000
Coghlan LF	1	0	0	0	0	0	.000
Ross PH-C	1	0	0	0	0	0	.000
Totals	49	5	10	5	4	12	

Giants	AB	R	H	RBI	BB	SO	AVG.
Span CF	6	2	2	0	0	1	.200
Belt 1B	4	1	1	1	1	1	.200
Posey C	5	1	3	1	1	0	.385
Pence RF	6	0	1	0	0	2	.214
Gillaspie 3B	6	1	1	2	0	1	.182
Crawford SS	6	1	2	1	0	1	.231
Panik 2B	4	0	3	1	2	0	.571
Blanco LF	4	0	0	0	0	1	.200
Bumgarner P	1	0	0	0	0	0	.000
Núñez PH	1	0	0	0	0	0	.000
Law P	0	0	0	0	0	0	.000
Tomlinson PH	1	0	0	0	0	0	.000
Strickland P	0	0	0	0	0	0	.000
Hernández PH	1	0	0	0	0	0	.200
Romo P	0	0	0	0	0	0	.000
Smith P	0	0	0	0	0	0	.000
Brown PH	1	0	0	0	0	0	.000
Blach P	0	0	0	0	0	0	.000
Totals	33	5	9	5	1	6	

Cubs	IP	H	R	ER	BB	SO	HR	ERA
Arrieta	6.0	6	2	2	1	5	0	3.00
Strop (H, 1)	0.2	0	0	0	0	0	0	0.00
Wood (H, 1)	0.1	1	1	1	0	0	0	5.40
Rondón	0.0	0	1	1	1	0	0	13.50
Chapman (B, 1)	0.1	2	1	1	1	1	0	3.86
Grimm	0.2	0	0	0	0	0	0	0.00
Montgomery (L, 0-1)	4.0	4	1	1	1	1	0	1.69
Totals	12.0	13	6	6	4	7	0	

Giants	IP	H	R	ER	BB	SO	HR	ERA
Bumgarner	5.0	7	3	3	1	4	1	5.40
Law	2.0	0	0	0	1	2	0	0.00
Strickland	1.0	0	0	0	1	2	0	0.00
Romo (B, 1)	2.0	1	2	2	1	2	1	9.00
Smith	1.0	0	0	0	0	1	0	0.00
Blach (W, 1-0)	2.0	2	0	0	0	1	0	0.00
Totals	13.0	10	5	5	4	12	2	

Javier Baez delivers a clutch run-scoring single in the ninth inning. *AP Photo*

Is This The Year?
Cubs Rally In 9th

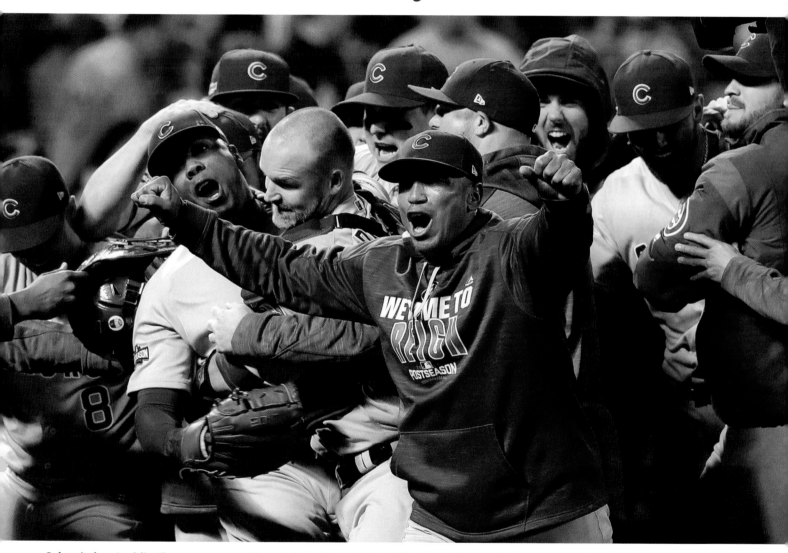

Cubs pitcher Aroldis Chapman, second from left, and catcher David Ross, celebrate with teammates after snapping the Giants playoff win streak. The Cubs now move on to the National League Championship Series. *AP Photo*

by GORDON WITTENMYER

Bring on Bryce Harper and Daniel Murphy. Or Corey Seager and Clayton Kershaw. Doesn't seem to matter to these Cubs who's next. Or when, or where, or how long it takes.

If they can make quick work of Madison Bumgarner one night and rally in the ninth on the next to eliminate the Giants in an even-numbered year, maybe next year really is here for the star-crossed franchise.

"It's a validation. It's everything that I believe that we are," manager Joe Maddon said after his club rallied for four ninth-inning runs against five different Giants relievers – with Javy Baez driving in the game winner with a single up the middle on an 0-2 pitch with one out.

"It was a tough game [Monday] night," said

David Ross is congratulated by starting pitcher John Lackey after hitting a solo home run during the third inning. *AP Photo*

Maddon of a 13-inning loss that included a blown save. "Things weren't going our way tonight. But we played nine innings hard and came out on top in a really difficult environment against a team that hasn't lost a closeout game in a while."

The Cubs snapped the Giants' 10-game winning streak in postseason elimination games, dating to 2012.

Up next is a Game 1 date Saturday with either the Dodgers or the Nationals in the National League Championship Series. It's the second consecutive trip to the NLCS for the Cubs who have won postseason series in back-to-back seasons for the first time since their World Series titles in 1907 and 1908.

"We're excited for it," said Kris Bryant, whose leadoff single started the ninth-inning rally. "A lot of us have a sour taste in our mouth from last year. We'll be ready for it and can't wait."

The Cubs were swept by the Mets in the NLCS

last season. Since then, they signed postseason veterans Ben Zobrist, Jason Heyward and John Lackey as free agents and traded for 100-mph closer Aroldis Chapman to turn a contender into a 103-win team and this year's World Series favorites.

One night after the closer acquired for October blew a save chance, Lackey trailed three batters into his start and never led – putting the Cubs on the brink of a return trip to Wrigley Field for a decisive Game 5 in a series they led 2-0.

"It's never a good feeling when we're not ourselves," said team president Theo Epstein, who was shown at times on the game broadcast not appearing to enjoy himself as the Giants lefty Matt Moore held the Cubs to two hits through eight innings to hand off a 5-2 lead.

"I knew we were going to snap out of it," Epstein said. "We wanted to get it done here, and our boys showed up when it mattered most."

Game 4 starting pitcher John Lackey went four innings allowing three earned runs while ringing up four strike outs. *AP Photo*

BOX SCORE

	1	2	3	4	5	6	7	8	9	R	H	E
Chicago	0	0	1	0	1	0	0	0	4	6	6	0
San Francisco	1	0	0	2	2	0	0	0	0	5	11	2

Cubs	AB	R	H	RBI	BB	SO	AVG.
Fowler CF	3	0	0	0	1	2	.133
Rondón P	0	0	0	0	0	0	.000
Chapman P	0	0	0	0	0	0	.000
Bryant 3B	4	1	1	0	0	2	.375
Rizzo 1B	2	1	1	0	2	1	.067
Zobrist LF-2B	4	1	1	1	0	1	.188
Russell SS	3	0	0	0	0	0	.067
Coghlan PH	0	0	0	0	0	0	.000
Contreras PH-LF	1	0	1	2	0	0	.667
Heyward RF-CF	4	1	0	0	0	1	.083
Báez 2B-SS	4	1	1	1	0	0	.375
Ross C	3	1	1	2	0	1	.167
Lackey P	1	0	0	0	0	1	.000
Almora Jr. PH	1	0	0	0	0	1	.000
Grimm P	0	0	0	0	0	0	.000
Wood P	0	0	0	0	0	0	1.000
Edwards Jr. P	0	0	0	0	0	0	.000
Soler PH-RF	1	0	0	0	0	0	.000
Totals	31	6	6	6	3	10	

Giants	AB	R	H	RBI	BB	SO	AVG.
Span CF	5	1	2	1	0	2	.267
Belt 1B	5	0	0	0	0	1	.133
Posey C	2	0	0	1	1	0	.333
Pence RF	4	1	1	0	0	1	.222
Crawford SS	4	1	1	0	0	2	.235
Gillaspie 3B	4	1	4	1	0	0	.400
Panik 2B	3	1	2	1	0	1	.600
Blanco LF	3	0	0	0	1	1	.125
Strickland P	0	0	0	0	0	0	.000
Moore P	3	0	1	1	0	1	.333
Law P	0	0	0	0	0	0	.000
López P	0	0	0	0	0	0	.000
Romo P	0	0	0	0	0	0	.000
Smith P	0	0	0	0	0	0	.000
Hernández LF	1	0	0	0	0	1	.167
Totals	34	5	11	5	2	10	

Cubs	IP	H	R	ER	BB	SO	HR	ERA
Lackey	4.0	7	3	3	2	4	0	6.75
Grimm	0.1	2	2	2	0	0	0	18.00
Wood	1.2	1	0	0	0	2	0	2.70
Edwards Jr.	1.0	0	0	0	0	0	0	0.00
Rondón (W, 1-0)	1.0	1	0	0	0	1	0	5.40
Chapman (S, 3)	1.0	0	0	0	0	3	0	2.70
Totals	9.0	11	5	5	2	10	0	

Giants	IP	H	R	ER	BB	SO	HR	ERA
Moore	8.0	2	2	1	2	10	1	1.13
Law	0.0	1	1	1	0	0	0	3.86
López	0.0	0	1	1	1	0	0	13.50
Romo	0.0	1	1	1	0	0	0	13.50
Smith (L, 0-1; B, 1)	0.1	1	1	0	0	0	0	0.00
Strickland	0.2	1	0	0	0	0	0	0.00
Totals	9.0	6	6	4	3	10	1	

After Bryant's single in the ninth and a pitching change, Anthony Rizzo walked. After another pitching change, Ben Zobrist doubled home a run. Then another pitching change, and pinch hitter Willson Contreras tied it with a single up the middle.

One out and another pitching change later, Baez drove his hit up the middle. And the young infielder who had been a conspicuous, celebrating thorn in the Giants' side the whole series celebrated again with an exaggerated clapping that seemed directed at the crowd.

If there was a NLDS MVP Baez would get it. "Absolutely," Maddon said. "How could he not be? He should get the Corvette."∎

Reigning National League Rookie
of the Year Kris Bryant. *AP Photo*

Kris Bryant 'On To Bigger And Better Things' Since Controversial Demotion

by **GORDON WITTENMYER**

Eleven months ago, Kris Bryant went from the best player in any spring training camp in baseball to the worst emotional place of his spring in the span of one early-morning meeting with Cubs officials.

Teammate Anthony Rizzo quietly consoled him with a simple thought: "Fast-forward a year, and everything you're going through, which is the biggest thing in your life right now, is not going to mean a thing to you anymore."

Yeah. Whatever.

But then the fast-forward thing happened. And almost as soon as Rizzo and Bryant got together for the first time in Mesa this spring, Rizzo said to him: "See what I mean?"

Bryant, now the reigning National League Rookie of the Year in the heart of the Cubs' batting order, is at the other end of the spring training universe this year.

"It's hard to even put thought into it now, just because it's so far away, so far in the past," he said. "I figured this year in spring training I would get asked questions about it, but for me I've moved on to bigger and better things."

Of course, it wasn't that easy, not for at least for a few days after the morning meeting, when he was cut from big-league camp despite the best offensive spring training in the majors in at least a decade.

Bryant, the No. 1 prospect in baseball entering camp last year, was told he had a chance to win a big-league job if he performed well enough, even though it seemed obvious from the beginning that he would open in the minors to delay the start of his service-time clock, thereby delaying free agency by a year.

For that to happen, he needed to spend 12 days in the minors. He was called up on the 13th day of the season.

It was the top story in baseball for multiple news cycles, especially as Bryant's agent, Scott Boras, spoke out.

It was such a conspicuous case of the kind of service-time manipulation that's common in the game that the players' union issued a rare statement decrying the move, and then filed a grievance, which remains unresolved as the union and owners head into a collective bargaining season.

Manager Joe Maddon has had more pleasant meetings with players than the one 11 months ago with Bryant.

"He was straight up with me," Maddon said, "looked me right in the eyeballs, and he was very self-confident."

And Bryant told the manager the team was wrong. That he deserved the job.

"And I don't blame him," Maddon said. "And then when he got up here he showed that that was true."

Bryant batted cleanup his first day in the majors. The third baseman started a game in center field six days later. He made the All-Star team. He hit home runs off Clayton Kershaw, Jacob deGrom and the left-field video board (on the way to 26 total). And he was the unanimous Rookie of the Year choice in one of the deepest rookie-class years in history.

"I was interested to see [how he would respond to the demotion]," Maddon said. "I was also confident that he would respond well."

Maybe it was Rizzo's advice. Or an angry passion that came out of that morning meeting 11 months ago. Or, as Bryant suggested, something he learned over three years at the University of San Diego.

Either way, "I just looked at it like I did everything I could," he said of regrouping emotionally. "I got over it pretty quick."

He homered in his first minor-league spring game after getting sent down.

"It's about learning to forget the past and live in the present and not really worry about the future," he said. "I honestly can say that I did that. And I think I'd grade myself an A-plus in that area." ∎

Miguel Montero watches his game-winning pinch hit grand slam leave the park. *AP Photo*

Montero Grand Slam Lifts Cubs Over Dodgers In Opener

Cubs catcher David Ross tags out Dodgers first baseman Adrian Gonzalez at home plate as starting pitcher Jon Lester looks on during the second inning. *AP Photo*

by GORDON WITTENMYER

If the Cubs are going to do this thing they've spent 108 years trying to get done, maybe this is the only way it's going to happen.

The guy who screws up on the bases winds up stealing home instead of getting picked off. The closer the Cubs spent their top draft pick to acquire for these moments blows another save when he gets pressed into eighth-inning duty again.

And then the catcher who swore he thought the club was going to release him when he lost his starting job to a rookie comes off the bench for a grand slam in the bottom of the eighth inning.

And just like that, the Cubs beat the Dodgers 8-4 in the opener of the National League Championship Series on Saturday night at quaking Wrigley Field.

"Feels awesome," said Miguel Montero, who watched right-hander Joe Blanton walk pinch-hitter Chris Coghlan intentionally to load the bases ahead of him in the eighth with the score tied.

Two strikes later, Montero launched what proved to be the game-winner to the back of

WORLD SERIES CHAMPIONS

67

the right-field bleachers. And then Dexter Fowler added on with another homer on the next pitch for the final score.

Until the Cubs' five-run outburst, it looked like manager Joe Maddon's postseason habit of bringing his closer in with six outs to go might cost the Cubs a victory, like it did in a 13-inning loss to the Giants Monday night.

After Mike Montgomery allowed a leadoff single to Andrew Toles, Maddon went to Pedro Strop, who walked Howie Kendrick and gave up an infield single to Justin Turner to load the bases.

On came Chapman.

Out went the lead.

After strikeouts of Corey Seager and Yasiel Puig, first baseman Adrian Gonzalez drilled a two-run single through the box and up the middle to tie the game.

It was the second time this postseason a left-handed hitter had squared up a fastball from the lefty Chapman, who inexplicably did not use his slider in those at-bats.

"We had no choice. I did not want to do that again," Maddon said of bringing Chapman in with men on and six outs to go.

Until the bullpen carousel started up in the late innings, it looked like the Javy Baez Show for the second playoff series in a row.

The offensive and defensive hero of the Cubs' NLDS elimination of the Giants stepped to the plate for the first time Saturday, after Jason Heyward led off the second with a triple, to the

Cubs second baseman Javy Baez steals home during the second inning as Dodgers catcher Carlos Ruiz is unable to make the tag in time. *AP Photo*

Bill Murray cheers on the Cubs with his family. *AP Photo*

BOX SCORE

	1	2	3	4	5	6	7	8	9	R	H	E
Los Angeles	0	0	0	0	1	0	0	2	1	4	9	0
Chicago	1	2	0	0	0	0	0	5	-	8	9	0

Dodgers	AB	R	H	RBI	BB	SO	AVG.
Kendrick LF	3	0	0	0	0	0	.000
Utley PH-2B	1	1	0	0	1	0	.000
Turner 3B	4	0	1	0	0	0	.250
Seager SS	4	0	1	0	0	2	.250
Puig RF	4	0	0	0	0	1	.000
Blanton P	0	0	0	0	0	0	.000
Dayton P	0	0	0	0	0	0	.000
González 1B	4	0	2	2	0	1	.500
Ruiz C	2	0	0	0	0	0	.000
Grandal PH-C	2	0	0	0	0	1	.000
Hernández 2B-RF	2	0	0	0	2	0	.000
Pederson CF	4	1	1	0	0	2	.250
Maeda P	1	0	1	0	0	0	1.000
Ethier PH	1	1	1	1	0	0	1.000
Báez P	0	0	0	0	0	0	.000
Stripling P	0	0	0	0	0	0	.000
Toles PH-LF	2	1	2	1	0	0	1.000
Totals	34	4	9	4	3	7	

Cubs	AB	R	H	RBI	BB	SO	AVG.
Fowler CF	5	2	2	1	0	1	.400
Bryant 3B	4	0	2	1	1	0	.500
Rizzo 1B	5	0	0	0	0	2	.000
Zobrist LF	3	1	1	0	1	0	.333
Russell SS	4	0	0	0	0	1	.000
Heyward RF	3	2	1	0	1	0	.333
Báez 2B	4	1	2	1	0	0	.500
Ross C	3	0	0	0	0	1	.000
Coghlan PH	0	1	0	0	1	0	1.000
Contreras C	0	0	0	0	0	0	.000
Lester P	0	0	0	0	2	0	.000
Soler PH	1	0	0	0	0	0	.000
Wood P	0	0	0	0	0	0	.000
Edwards Jr. PO	0	0	0	0	0	0	.000
Montgomery P	0	0	0	0	0	0	.000
Strop PO	0	0	0	0	0	0	.000
Chapman P	0	0	0	0	0	0	.000
Montero PH	1	1	1	4	0	0	1.000
Rondón PO	0	0	0	0	0	0	.000
Totals	33	8	9	7	6	5	

Dodgers	IP	H	R	ER	BB	SO	HR	ERA
Maeda	4.0	4	3	3	3	2	0	6.75
Báez	2.0	1	0	0	1	3	0	0.00
Stripling	1.0	0	0	0	0	0	0	0.00
Blanton (L, 0-1)	0.2	4	5	5	2	0	2	67.50
Dayton	0.1	0	0	0	0	0	0	0.00
Totals	8.0	9	8	8	6	5	2	

Cubs	IP	H	R	ER	BB	SO	HR	ERA
Lester	6.0	4	1	1	1	3	1	1.50
Wood (H, 1)	0.1	0	0	0	0	0	0	0.00
Edwards Jr. (H, 1)	0.1	0	0	0	1	1	0	0.00
Montgomery (H, 1)	0.1	1	1	1	0	1	0	27.00
Strop	0.0	1	1	1	1	0	0	---
Chapman (W, 1-0; B, 1)	1.0	1	0	0	0	2	0	0.00
Rondón	1.0	2	1	1	0	0	0	9.00
Totals	9.0	9	4	4	3	7	1	

chants from 43,000 fans of "Ja-vy!" "Ja-vy!"

He didn't disappoint on that one, turning a popup hit to shallow left-center into a double by breaking out of the box like he didn't do at home in either of the first two games of the last series.

But the big play came after he advanced to third on a wild pitch and, with the squeeze play on, wound up with the Cubs' first postseason stolen base since 1907.

Jon Lester pulled the bat back on the bunt, and with Baez well down the line, catcher Carlos Ruiz threw to third as Baez simultaneously broke for the plate. He slid just under the ensuing throw back to the plate.

"You've got to have some cajones to pull that off," Ross said.■

Dodgers starting pitcher Clayton Kershaw in the middle of his unorthodox windup. Kershaw threw a two-hitter over seven innings in the Dodgers 1-0 win. *AP Photo*

After Game 2 Victory, Kershaw Looms Over The Cubs

Cubs shortstop Addison Russell tags out Dodgers first baseman Adrian Gonzalez for a double play during the sixth inning.
AP Photo

by RICK MORRISSEY

Well before he took the mound Sunday night, Clayton Kershaw was hanging darkly over the National League Championship Series for the Cubs.

Kershaw pitched fabulously in Game 2 at Wrigley Field, could pitch Game 5 in Los Angeles and might be available in some capacity for Game 7, *if necessary and *if the sky is falling for the Cubs.

He is a possible boogeyman in this series, and he looked every bit of it Sunday in a 1-0 Dodgers' victory that tied the series at a game apiece. That herky-jerky motion and those four disparate

pitches had hitters baffled too often. The Cubs didn't get a hit until the fifth inning. You don't want to dismiss such dominance as inconsequential, but it really was all prelude. Everyone was tapping a foot impatiently to see if Clayton Kershaw, regular-season killer, would revert to Clayton Kershaw, postseason pacifist.

Going into Sunday's game, he had a 3-6 career playoff record. That included a 0-3 record and a 7.23 earned-run average in the NLCS. Not what you'd expect from a three-time Cy Young winner.

He gave up two hits over seven innings before his night was done. It might not have been as

WORLD SERIES CHAMPIONS

loud as Miguel Montero's grand slam in Game 1, but it was loud enough.

Talk to two different Cubs hitters and hear two different explanations about what went wrong at the plate in Game 2. That's how good, and confusing, Kershaw was Sunday.

"You just know that he's going to come in and throw strikes," first baseman Anthony Rizzo said. "You're going to sit back and be 0-2 right away if that's the case, so you've got to be ready to hit."

"We just chased a lot of pitches," second baseman Javy Baez said. "I honestly thought with him pitching with a couple days' rest, he wasn't going to be that nasty. Obviously, he came ready for us."

Kershaw started Game 4 of the division series against the Nationals, throwing 110 pitches, then came back two days later to get the save in Game 5 and propel the Dodgers into the NLCS. And now here he was three days after that, hoping to change the complexion of the championship series with a good outing. The Cubs were hoping for a tired pitcher. They got power and adrenaline.

Kershaw struck out Baez on a 95 m.p.h. fastball in the second inning, so, no, arm fatigue didn't look like it was going to be an issue. Rizzo got ahold of a pitch in the fourth but it was foul. Ben Zobrist hit one hard in the fifth, but Dodgers left fielder Andrew Toles caught it on the warning track.

BOX SCORE

	1	2	3	4	5	6	7	8	9		R	H	E
Los Angeles	0	1	0	0	0	0	0	0	0		1	3	1
Chicago	0	0	0	0	0	0	0	0	0		0	2	0

Dodgers	AB	R	H	RBI	BB	SO	AVG.
Utley 2B	3	0	0	0	1	2	.000
Seager SS	3	0	0	0	1	1	.143
Turner 3B	2	0	0	0	1	0	.167
González 1B	3	1	1	1	1	1	.429
Reddick RF	4	0	1	0	0	0	.250
Jansen P	0	0	0	0	0	0	.000
Pederson CF	3	0	0	0	1	0	.143
Grandal C	1	0	0	0	2	0	.000
Toles LF	2	0	0	0	0	1	.500
Hernández PH-LF	2	0	0	0	0	0	.000
Kershaw P	3	0	1	0	0	1	.333
Puig RF	1	0	0	0	0	0	.000
Totals	27	1	3	1	7	6	

Cubs	AB	R	H	RBI	BB	SO	AVG.
Fowler CF	4	0	0	0	0	1	.222
Bryant 3B	4	0	0	0	0	2	.250
Rizzo 1B	3	0	0	0	1	0	.000
Zobrist LF	3	0	0	0	0	1	.167
Russell SS	3	0	0	0	0	0	.000
Báez 2B	3	0	1	0	0	1	.429
Contreras C	3	0	1	0	0	2	.333
Heyward RF	3	0	0	0	0	0	.167
Hendricks P	1	0	0	0	0	1	.000
Edwards Jr. P	0	0	0	0	0	0	.000
Soler PH	1	0	0	0	0	1	.000
Montgomery P	0	0	0	0	0	0	.000
Strop P	0	0	0	0	0	0	.000
Montero PH	1	0	0	0	0	1	.500
Chapman P	0	0	0	0	0	0	.000
Totals	29	0	2	0	1	10	

Dodgers	IP	H	R	ER	BB	SO	HR	ERA
Kershaw (W, 1-0)	7.0	2	0	0	1	6	0	0.00
Jansen (S, 1)	2.0	0	0	0	0	4	0	0.00
Totals	9.0	2	0	0	1	10	0	

Cubs	IP	H	R	ER	BB	SO	HR	ERA
Hendricks (L, 0-1)	5.1	3	1	1	4	5	1	1.69
Edwards Jr.	0.2	0	0	0	0	0	0	0.00
Montgomery	1.0	0	0	0	2	1	0	6.75
Strop	1.0	0	0	0	0	0	0	9.00
Chapman	1.0	0	0	0	1	0	0	0.00
Totals	9.0	3	1	1	7	6	1	

Baez broke up the no-hitter with a two-out single. Willson Conteras followed with a single up the middle. The crowd of 42,384 started to get ideas. But then light-hitting Jason Heyward ended the inning with a pop-out to third. Perhaps you saw that coming.

It was a terrific pitching duel, with Adrian Gonzalez' solo homer off the Cubs' Kyle Hendricks in the second the difference.

"The way Hendricks was throwing, it was one of those games where one pitch could have been the deciding factor," Kershaw said.■

Dodgers starting pitcher Rich Hill delivers to the plate during Game 3. *AP Photo*

Hollywood Scuffle: Cubs Shut Out Again By Dodgers

Dodgers right fielder Josh Reddick beats the tag of Cubs second baseman Javier Baez as he steals second base during the fourth inning. *AP Photo*

by GORDON WITTENMYER

The Cubs saw some of this coming in August.

To be clear, nobody in the Cubs' clubhouse saw Tuesday night's 6-0 loss to reinvented ex-Cub Rich Hill and the Dodgers in Game 3 of the National League Championship Series.

But the Cubs saw a tough playoff rematch looming when they left Dodger Stadium in August after struggling for three games against the Dodgers' pitching – without having faced Clayton Kershaw all year.

"We would have our hands full because of all the lefties they have," Ben Zobrist said at the conclusion of that series.

WORLD SERIES CHAMPIONS

75

Cubs outfielders Dexter Fowler, left, and Jorge Soler collide on a fly ball during the third inning. Fowler was able to hang on and make the catch. *AP Photo*

By the time one of those lefties, Hill, was through six scoreless innings Tuesday, Zobrist had never looked more like a swami. And by the time Kenley Jansen retired Chris Coghlan on a liner to third for the final out, the Cubs' lineup looked lost.

They haven't scored since Miguel Montero and Dexter Fowler's back-to-back homers in the eighth inning of Saturday's Game 1, and they face hard-throwing rookie left-hander Julio Urias on Wednesday, trailing 2-1 in the best-of-seven series.

"There's no panic in here," Kris Bryant said.

Easy for him to say. He had both hits against Hill, and he's been the best-hitting Cub in the postseason (10-for-28).

This is uncharted 2016 territory for the Cubs: The first time this year they've been shut out in back-to-back games - first time since August they've been shut out at all.

The part that's not uncharted is this: That last team to shut them out was the Dodgers. In fact, the Dodgers have four of the eight shutouts pitched against the Cubs this year.

"We may be a little unhappy about how the game transpired," said Cubs starter Jake Arrieta, who gave up a pair of costly home runs but otherwise pitched well into the sixth inning. "But guys will get back to their families at the hotel and decompress and prepare for tomorrow."

Either way, they're going to have to try to find a way to beat a Dodgers lefty at least once in the next two days to assure a return to Wrigley Field for a Game 6. Kershaw's in the wings for Game 5 if the Dodgers decide they need him on short rest.

Zobrist and teammates have known for nearly two months how tough that was going to be.

"They pitch up with their heater in the zone, and they've been pretty solid staying in the strike zone with those, and just above the strike zone," Zobrist said during Monday's workout day.

Hill with his slow curve kept the Cubs at bay with little in the way of a scoring chance — helping beat the Cubs in the playoffs for the second time in his career. He lasted just three innings in a 2007 Division Series loss to the Diamondbacks.

Hill, who was pitching for the independent Long Island Ducks barely a year ago, had a runner in scoring position against him only once, in the second after a pair of walks. Beyond that he gave up a two-out single to Kris Bryant in the third and a one-out single to Bryant in the sixth. ▪

BOX SCORE

	1	2	3	4	5	6	7	8	9		R	H	E
Chicago	0	0	0	0	0	0	0	0	0		0	4	0
Los Angeles	0	0	1	2	0	1	0	2	-		6	10	0

Cubs	AB	R	H	RBI	BB	SO	AVG.
Fowler CF	4	0	1	0	0	0	.231
Bryant 3B	4	0	2	0	0	2	.333
Zobrist LF-2B	4	0	0	0	0	0	.100
Rizzo 1B	3	0	1	0	1	1	.091
Báez 2B-SS	4	0	0	0	0	1	.273
Soler RF	1	0	0	0	1	1	.000
Coghlan PH-LF	2	0	0	0	0	0	.000
Russell SS	2	0	0	0	0	1	.000
Heyward PH-RF	1	0	0	0	0	1	.143
Montero C	2	0	0	0	0	0	.250
Contreras PH-C	1	0	0	0	0	1	.250
Arrieta P	2	0	0	0	0	2	.000
Wood P	0	0	0	0	0	0	.000
Grimm P	0	0	0	0	0	0	.000
Almora Jr. PH	1	0	0	0	0	0	.000
Montgomery P	0	0	0	0	0	0	.000
Totals	31	0	4	0	2	10	

Dodgers	AB	R	H	RBI	BB	SO	AVG.
Utley 2B	4	0	0	0	0	1	.000
Jansen P	0	0	0	0	0	0	.000
Seager SS	4	0	3	1	0	1	.364
Turner 3B	4	1	1	1	0	1	.200
González 1B	4	0	0	0	0	1	.273
Reddick RF	2	1	1	0	0	0	.333
a-Puig PH-RF	2	1	2	0	0	0	.286
Pederson CF	4	1	1	1	0	2	.182
Grandal C	3	1	1	3	1	1	.167
Toles LF	2	1	1	0	0	0	.500
Kendrick PH-LF-2B	2	0	0	0	0	1	.000
Hill P	2	0	0	0	0	0	.000
Blanton P	0	0	0	0	0	0	.000
Ethier PH1	0	0	0	0	0	2	.500
Dayton P	0	0	0	0	0	0	.000
Hernández LF	0	0	0	0	0	0	.000
Totals	34	6	10	6	1	8	

Cubs	IP	H	R	ER	BB	SO	HR	ERA
Arrieta (L, 0-1)	5.0	6	4	4	0	5	2	7.20
Wood	0.2	1	0	0	1	1	0	0.00
Grimm	1.1	1	0	0	0	1	0	0.00
Montgomery	1.0	2	2	2	0	1	0	11.57
Totals	8.0	10	6	6	1	8	2	

Dodgers	IP	H	R	ER	BB	SO	HR	ERA
Hill (W, 1-0)	6.0	2	0	0	2	6	0	0.00
Blanton	1.0	1	0	0	0	1	0	27.00
Dayton	0.2	1	0	0	0	1	0	0.00
Jansen	1.1	1	0	0	0	2	0	0.00
Totals	9.0	4	0	0	2	10	0	

Anthony Rizzo is congratulated by teammate, Javy Baez, after connecting on a fifth inning home run. *AP Photo*

CHICAGO CUBS 10 • LOS ANGELES DODGERS 2

Cubs Even NLCS 2-2
As Bats Break Out

Cubs shortstop Addison Russell hits a two-run home run in the fourth inning. *AP Photo*

by GORDON WITTENMYER

If this is the way it's going to be the rest of the way, Cubs fans are in for the postseason thrill ride of their lives. Or in need of prescription-strength Dramamine by Sunday.

A 10-2 victory by the Cubs at Dodger Stadium in Game 4 Wednesday night evened the National League Championship Series at two games apiece, assuring a return to Wrigley Field for a Game 6.

But that's the only thing that seems remotely assured as this series heads to a pivotal Game 5 Thursday night, considering the way it has played out so far – not to mention the drama surrounding the looming Clayton Kershaw.

"It's been a pretty interesting series to this point," Cubs manager Joe Maddon said. "It's two out of three right now. I think it's great. I think it's great for baseball. It's very exciting stuff."

On this night it was all Cubs from the fourth inning on, against 20-year-old rookie left-hander Julio Urias and the Dodger bullpen.

WORLD SERIES CHAMPIONS

79

"It's huge," said Addison Russell, whose two-run homer in the fourth capped a four-run inning - after 21 consecutive scoreless innings through Wednesday's third.

"Especially [Anthony] Rizzo and I with pretty big nights," said Russell, who was 1-for-25 this postseason before the homer. "And just overall, everyone - I mean, 13 hits is huge in the playoffs."

Rizzo, borrowing a move – and a bat – he used several times down the stretch and even Tuesday night, took teammate Matt Szczur's same-size, different-model lumber after striking out in his first two at-bats Wednesday.

The result: three hits and three RBIs the rest of the night, including a homer leading off the fifth in his first turn with the bat.

"I'm just trying to help the team anyway I can," said Szczur, who is traveling with the team but not on the playoff roster.

"The first two at-bats weren't so hot," said Rizzo of the impetus for the switch on this night. "It worked."

He was 2-for-28 with two singles and nine strikeouts until then.

The outburst marked the biggest high for the Cubs playoff run since Miguel Montero's pinch grand slam for the Game 1 victory in Saturday's eighth inning.

It all started in the fourth as a snowball rolling downhill.

Cubs catcher Willson Contreras tags out the Dodgers Adrian Gonzalez on a close play at home during the second inning. After an umpires review, the call stood. *AP Photo*

BOX SCORE

	1	2	3	4	5	6	7	8	9	R	H	E
Chicago	0	0	0	4	1	5	0	0	0	10	13	2
Los Angeles	0	0	0	0	2	0	0	0	0	2	6	4

Cubs	AB	R	H	RBI	BB	SO	AVG.
Fowler CF	5	1	2	1	0	0	.278
Bryant 3B	2	1	0	0	2	1	.286
Rizzo 1B	5	2	3	3	0	2	.250
Zobrist LF	5	1	2	0	0	0	.200
Báez 2B	3	1	1	1	1	0	.286
Contreras C	5	1	1	1	0	2	.222
Heyward RF	5	0	0	1	0	2	.083
Russell SS	5	2	3	2	0	0	.214
Lackey P	2	0	0	0	0	1	.000
Montgomery P	1	1	1	0	0	0	1.000
Soler PH	1	0	0	0	0	0	.000
Edwards Jr. P	0	0	0	0	0	0	.000
Wood P	0	0	0	0	0	0	.000
Strop P	0	0	0	0	0	0	.000
Almora Jr. PH	1	0	0	0	0	0	.000
Rondón P	0	0	0	0	0	0	.000
Totals	40	10	13	9	3	8	

Dodgers	AB	R	H	RBI	BB	SO	AVG.
Utley 2B	2	0	0	0	0	0	.000
Kendrick PH-LF-2B	3	0	1	0	0	1	.125
Seager SS	3	0	0	0	1	1	.286
Turner 3B	3	0	1	2	1	1	.231
González 1B	4	0	1	0	0	0	.267
Wood P	0	0	0	0	0	0	.000
Reddick RF	1	0	0	0	0	0	.286
Hernández PH-2B	1	0	0	0	0	0	.000
Avilán P	0	0	0	0	0	0	.000
Ruiz C	1	0	0	0	0	1	.000
Pederson CF	4	0	1	0	0	2	.200
Grandal C-1B	3	0	0	0	1	1	.111
Toles LF-RF-LF	3	1	1	0	1	1	.444
Urías P	1	0	0	0	0	0	.000
Báez P	0	0	0	0	0	0	.000
Fields P	0	0	0	0	0	0	.000
Ethier PH	0	1	0	0	1	0	.500
Stripling P	0	0	0	0	0	0	.000
Puig RF	2	0	1	0	0	0	.333
Totals	31	2	6	2	5	8	

Cubs	IP	H	R	ER	BB	SO	HR	ERA
Lackey	4.0	3	2	2	3	3	0	4.50
Montgomery (W, 1-0)	2.0	2	0	0	0	2	0	6.23
Edwards Jr.	0.2	0	0	0	1	1	0	0.00
Wood	0.1	0	0	0	1	0	0	0.00
Strop	1.0	0	0	0	0	1	0	4.50
Rondón	1.0	1	0	0	0	1	0	4.50
Totals	9.0	6	2	2	5	8	0	

Dodgers	IP	H	R	ER	BB	SO	HR	ERA
Urías (L, 0-1)	3.2	4	4	4	2	4	1	9.82
Báez	0.2	2	1	1	0	1	1	3.38
Fields	0.2	0	0	0	0	1	0	0.00
Stripling	0.1	4	5	4	1	0	0	27.00
Avilán	1.2	1	0	0	0	1	0	0.00
Wood	2.0	2	0	0	0	1	0	0.00
Totals	9.0	13	10	9	3	8	2	

A Cubs lineup hitting just .185 this postseason and averaging three runs a game, got started on Ben Zobrist's fourth-inning bunt toward third that died on the grass for a leadoff single without a throw.

Then came a bloop to left by Javy Baez, followed by a soft liner to left from Willson Contreras, and the Cubs had their first run since Saturday.

Jason Heyward drove in a run with a grounder, followed by Russell's homer.

"It was fun to see our guys swing the bats well, a fun game to be a part of," said starter John Lackey, who was pulled from the game with a 5-0 lead after walking the first two batters in the fifth – angry enough to be seen muttering an expletive as manager Joe Maddon emerged from the dugout to get him.

"Up five runs, yeah," he said. "I was pretty surprised, but it was a great team win. Good to see our guys swing the bats well." ∎

Cubs starting pitcher Jon Lester delivered seven shutout innings in Game 5.   *AP Photo*

CHICAGO CUBS 8 • LOS ANGELES DODGERS 4

Cubs On Brink Of First World Series Since 1945

Cubs shortstop Addison Russell watches as his two-run home run off Dodgers relief pitcher Joe Blanton exits the stadium.
AP Photo

by GORDON WITTENMYER

Deciding against ace Clayton Kershaw for Game 5, the Dodgers instead sent out the ghosts against the Cubs on Thursday night at Dodger Stadium.

But Jon Lester was nine months old when Steve Garvey kept the Cubs out of the World Series in 1984. And Addison Russell was in fourth grade when Eric Karros stood at first base for the double-play relay that never came in that fateful eighth inning in 2003.

How do you believe in ghosts when you can't see them?

By the time Garvey and Karros got done whipping the Dodger Stadium crowd into a

WORLD SERIES CHAMPIONS

Cubs second baseman Javy Baez makes an incredible bare-handed play on a Adrian Gonzalez bunt during the seventh inning. Gonzalez was out on a bang-bang play at first. *AP Photo*

pregame frenzy with a surprise introduction of broadcasting legend Vin Scully, Lester and Russell quickly got to work putting the Cubs on the brink of silencing 71 years of much bigger franchise ghosts.

Lester continued his October of dominance for the Cubs with seven more shutdown innings, and Russell hit his second big home run in as many nights as the Cubs beat the Dodgers 8-4 to take a commanding 3-2 lead in the best-of-seven National League Championship Series.

"The city of Chicago's got to be buzzing pretty good right now," Cubs manager Joe Maddon said.

For the third time since 1945 – first since they were famously five outs away in 2003 – the Cubs are one victory from the World Series as they head home for Game 6 on Saturday night.

"Like Rizz said, it's gonna be epic," said third baseman Kris Bryant, who had two more hits in this one.

And if the apparent imminence of the first Cubs World Series since integration represents another historic hurdle – a target, even – Maddon said it's something his team plans to embrace like they did

Cubs manager Joe Maddon congratulates Aroldis Chapman and teammates following the NLCS Game 5 win. *AP Photo*

the favorite's target this season.

"That's been our goal all year," he said. "Now that we're very close to it, I want us to go out and play the same game. I want to go after it like, `Lets just go play our Saturday game and see how it falls.' "

The Cubs backed up Lester's shutdown pitching with seven late-inning runs to rout the Dodgers for the second consecutive game after falling behind 2-1 in the series.

Lester, who started both Game 1 victories for the Cubs this postseason, went seven strong, allowing just one in the fourth, never trailing.

Russell, who snapped out of a postseason-long slump Wednesday, hit the two-run homer in the sixth that put the Cubs ahead, before they added five more in a sloppy eighth inning by the Dodgers.

"Just rounding the bases it was pretty exciting," Russell said. "I was pumped up not only for myself but for the team and the little cushion Jonny had

to go from there."

Lester allowed just five hits and one walk.

Cubs postseason star Javy Baez made the defensive play of the game on Adrian Gonzalez's bunt past the mound in the seventh – bare-handing and throwing in one motion to get Gonzalez by a half-step (after a replay challenge overturned a safe call).

Then he added a three-run double in the eighth – coming up limping briefly after turning his ankle slightly rounding second.

He stayed in the game and said afterward he was fine.

"These guys won the game for us tonight," Lester said of Russell and Baez. "I was just kind of along for the ride.■

Co-MVP's of the NLCS, Jon Lester and Javy Baez, celebrate the Cubs return to the World Series. *AP Photo*

World Series Bound: 'This Is A New Cubs Team'

Cubs players celebrate reaching the World Series for the first time in 71 years. *AP Photo*

by GORDON WITTENMYER

These aren't your father's Cubs. Or your grandfather's – or his goat's.

Maybe one day next month or next spring – after Addison Russell, Kris Bryant and Javy Baez have had a chance to rest up from a month in their personal October sandbox – they might even realize it themselves.

Until then, know only this: Next year finally arrived for the Cubs, at roughly 9:45 p.m.

Saturday night – just 71 years and 12 days since the last time they saw a pitch in the World Series.

"We don't care about history," said Bryant after he drove in the first run in a 5-0 victory over the Dodgers in the National League Championship Series clincher that shook Wrigley Field to its newly poured foundation.

"This is a completely different team," Bryant said. "Different people all around. It don't

WORLD SERIES CHAMPIONS

matter. This is a new Chicago Cubs team. And we're certainly a very confident group."

Different? Confident? Kyle Hendricks outpitched three-time Cy Young winner Clayton Kershaw with 7 1/3 near-flawless innings, and the youngest lineup to ever take the field in a league championship series clincher did the rest to propel the Cubs to their first World Series since 1945.

"There's another trophy we want," said general manager Jed Hoyer, who came in with team president Theo Epstein in the fall of 2011 and began a full rebuild. "You take a little bit of time to appreciate doing something that hasn't been done in 71 years--you look at the way these people are celebrating, and it's awesome.

"But we're not going to be satisfied," he said. "We want one more trophy; that's the goal. So you take tonight, you enjoy it, and then you get ready to win four more games."

If there was a downbeat note on this night of unbridled release by generations of fans who were packed 42,000 deep in the ballpark – and tens of thousands deeper in the surrounding streets and sidewalks – it was the

Cubs starting pitcher Kyle Hendricks receives a standing ovation from Cubs fans after allowing just two hits through seven innings. *AP Photo*

A goggled Kris Bryant lets loose in the post game locker room celebration. *AP Photo*

BOX SCORE

	1	2	3	4	5	6	7	8	9	R	H	E
Los Angeles	0	0	0	0	0	0	0	0	0	0	2	1
Chicago	2	1	0	1	1	0	0	0	-	5	7	1

Dodgers	AB	R	H	RBI	BB	SO	AVG.
Toles LF-CF	3	0	1	0	0	0	.462
Seager SS	3	0	0	0	0	1	.286
Turner 3B	3	0	0	0	0	0	.200
González 1B	3	0	0	0	0	0	.190
Reddick RF	3	0	1	0	0	0	.364
Pederson CF	2	0	0	0	0	2	.190
Kendrick PH-LF	1	0	0	0	0	0	.154
Grandal C	2	0	0	0	0	2	.083
Hernández PH	1	0	0	0	0	1	.000
Utley 2B	2	0	0	0	0	0	.000
Ruiz PH	0	0	0	0	1	0	.143
Kershaw P	1	0	0	0	0	1	.250
Ethier PH	1	0	0	0	0	0	.250
Jansen P	0	0	0	0	0	0	.000
Puig PH	1	0	0	0	0	0	.286
Totals	26	0	2	0	1	7	

Cubs	AB	R	H	RBI	BB	SO	AVG.
Fowler CF	4	1	2	1	0	2	.333
Bryant 3B	4	1	1	1	0	1	.304
Rizzo 1B	4	1	2	1	0	0	.320
Zobrist LF	3	0	0	1	0	1	.150
Heyward RF	0	0	0	0	0	0	.063
Báez 2B	3	0	0	0	0	1	.318
Contreras C	3	1	1	1	0	0	.286
Russell SS	3	1	1	0	0	1	.273
Almora Jr. RF-LF	3	0	0	0	0	1	.000
Hendricks P	3	0	0	0	0	1	.000
Chapman P	0	0	0	0	0	0	.000
Totals	30	5	7	5	0	8	

Dodgers	IP	H	R	ER	BB	SO	HR	ERA
Kershaw (L, 1-1)	5.0	7	5	4	0	4	2	3.00
Jansen	3.0	0	0	0	0	4	0	0.00
Totals	8.0	7	5	4	0	8	2	

Cubs	IP	H	R	ER	BB	SO	HR	ERA
Hendricks (W, 1-1)	7.1	2	0	0	0	6	0	0.71
Chapman	1.2	0	0	0	1	1	0	3.86
Totals	9.0	2	0	0	1	7	0	

moment manager Joe Maddon made the slow walk to the mound to pull Kyle Hendricks from the historic start.

Maddon, the first manager to take the Cubs to the World Series since Charlie Grimm, was booed by the full-house, full-throated crowd – which then quickly pivoted into a standing ovation for Hendricks.

Hendricks left the game after allowing his first hit since the first batter of the game – a one-out single by Josh Reddick in the eighth – as the public address system played his walkup music (Aerosmith's "Sweet Emotion") instead of incoming closer Aroldis Chapman's.

Hendricks retired 18 straight before the hit (including a pickoff to end the second).

Kershaw?

The greatest pitcher on earth succumbed to the biggest American sports story in a century as the Cubs jumped on the left-hander for two quick runs in the first and never looked back.

Lester, who started the Cubs' victories in Games 1 and 5 allowed just two hits in 13 innings, earned co-MVP honors for the series with defensive and offensive hero Baez.

"Listen, man, I know that we played a great, great team. And we're going to have to play another really great team," said front office special assistant Ryan Dempster, the Game 1 starter for the Cubs' 2008 playoff favorite. "But this group, they're special, man. I've been around a few. And they're special."■

CUBS

DON'T HAVE
A
KLUBER

#WAHOOBROTHERS

Kluber Shuts Down Cubs In World Series Opener

Cleveland Indians starting pitcher Corey Kluber set a World Series record with eight strikeouts in the first three innings. *AP Photo*

by GORDON WITTENMYER

It took forever for the Cubs to play in the World Series.

Make that forever and a day.

Indians starter Corey Kluber saw to that by shutting down the Cubs for much of a World Series opener that was 71 years in the making, beating the Cubs 6-0 Tuesday night at Progressive Field in Cleveland.

The Cubs managed just three hits against Kluber through the first six innings in support of their own postseason ace, Jon Lester.

And Indians manager Terry Francona

WORLD SERIES CHAMPIONS

93

Cubs designated hitter Kyle Schwarber doubles in the fourth inning. *AP Photo*

confirmed after the game he pulled Kluber one batter into the seventh because he plans to bring the 2014 Cy Young Award winner back on short rest for Game 4 – putting Kluber in position also for a possible Game 7.

Now what? Winners of Game 1 have won the last six World Series and 24 of the last 28.

"We got a long ways to go," said Lester, who referenced a lot of the gloom-and-doom chatter after the Cubs lost back-to-back shutouts to the Dodgers to fall behind 2-1 in the National League Championship Series.

"Everybody counted us out after Game 3," he said. "They said we were the 'worst best team in baseball.' We're here. We're not giving up. I'm not too worried about what guys say or anything like that. I know my guys."

After that Game 3 against the Dodgers, the Cubs scored 23 runs to sweep the next three games.

This one was more about Kluber – and two-inning bullpen ace Andrew Miller – than anything else.

"He was pretty much as dominant as one could be," Anthony Rizzo said of Kluber, whose eight strikeouts through three innings set a World Series record.

At least they had the celebrated return of Kyle Schwarber to help distract from the sting on this chilly night in Cleveland.

Schwarber, who had four hitless at-bats during the season before suffering a season-ending knee injury in the third game, returned to start Game 1 as the Cubs' designated hitter, batting fifth. He struck out on a 3-2 pitch in his first at-bat, but doubled off the right field wall against Kluber in the fourth and walked against Miller in the seventh.

Schwarber is the first non-pitcher in history to produce a hit in the World Series after going hitless during the regular season.

"You could see on the finish sometimes maybe the [knee] brace grabs him just a little bit," manager Joe Maddon said. "Otherwise, there was no kind of negative atmosphere surrounding his at-bats. I thought they were outstanding, actually."

BOX SCORE

	1	2	3	4	5	6	7	8	9		R	H	E
Chicago	0	0	0	0	0	0	0	0	0		0	7	0
Cleveland	2	0	1	0	0	0	0	3	-		6	10	0

Cubs	AB	R	H	RBI	BB	SO	AVG.
Fowler CF	4	0	0	0	0	2	.000
Bryant 3B	3	0	0	0	1	2	.000
Rizzo 1B	4	0	0	0	0	0	.000
Zobrist LF	4	0	3	0	0	0	.750
Schwarber DH	3	0	1	0	1	2	.333
Báez 2B	4	0	1	0	0	2	.250
Coghlan RF	2	0	0	0	0	2	.000
Contreras PH-C	2	0	1	0	0	0	.500
Russell SS	4	0	0	0	0	3	.000
Ross C	3	0	1	0	0	1	.333
Almora Jr. RF	0	0	0	0	0	0	.000
Montero PH	1	0	0	0	0	1	.000
Totals	34	0	7	0	2	15	

Indians	AB	R	H	RBI	BB	SO	AVG.
Davis CF	5	0	1	0	0	1	.200
Kipnis 2B	5	0	0	0	0	0	.000
Lindor SS	4	1	3	0	0	0	.750
Napoli 1B	3	1	0	0	1	2	.000
Santana DH	2	0	0	0	2	2	.000
Ramírez 3B	4	0	3	1	0	0	.750
Guyer LF	2	1	0	1	1	2	.000
Chisenhall RF	4	1	1	0	0	1	.250
Pérez C	4	2	2	4	0	1	.500
Totals	33	6	10	6	4	9	

Cubs	IP	H	R	ER	BB	SO	HR	ERA
Lester (L, 0-1)	5.2	6	3	3	3	7	1	4.76
Strop	0.2	0	0	0	0	1	0	0.00
Wood	0.1	0	0	0	0	0	0	0.00
Grimm	1.0	2	2	2	1	1	0	18.00
Rondón	0.1	2	1	1	0	0	1	27.00
Totals	8.0	10	6	6	4	9	2	

Indians	IP	H	R	ER	BB	SO	HR	ERA
Kluber (W, 1-0)	6.0	4	0	0	0	9	0	0.00
Miller (H, 1)	2.0	2	0	0	2	3	0	0.00
Allen	1.0	1	0	0	0	3	0	0.00
Totals	9.0	7	0	0	2	15	0	

The Cubs left the game optimistic over the fact they took Miller out of play for at least the next game by pushing his pitch count to a postseason high 46 in his two innings.

"That's good for us, and guys getting to see him in the first game I think is always to the hitter's advantage," Rizzo said. "I don't think anyone's hanging their head."

By the end of the game, after putting runners in scoring position in each of the last three innings (including bases loaded in the seventh), the Cubs seemed confident, if not upbeat heading into Arrieta's start Wednesday.

"We've got a lot of confidence in our guys," catcher David Ross said. "This is a resilient group." ∎

Cubs left fielder Ben Zobrist drills a RBI triple during the fifth inning.
AP Photo

World Series

GAME 2   OCTOBER 26, 2016   PROGRESSIVE FIELD   CLEVELAND, OHIO

CHICAGO CUBS 5 • CLEVELAND INDIANS 1

Arrieta, Bats Rock Cleveland As Cubs Even World Series

Cubs starting pitcher Jake Arrieta carried a no-hitter into the sixth inning of Game 2. *AP Photo*

by GORDON WITTENMYER

One night after making history just by showing up, the Cubs flirted Wednesday night with the kind of World Series history that only the Yankees have made.

They settled for a 5-1 victory over the Indians in Game 2 at Progressive Field, stealing the home-field advantage as the series shifts to Wrigley Field for Game 3 on Friday.

Shut out in Tuesday's opener, the Cubs peppered Indians starter Trevor Bauer and the Cleveland bullpen with nine hits and eight walks, taking a lead three batters into the game and

WORLD SERIES CHAMPIONS

C 97

First baseman Anthony Rizzo delivers a clutch first inning RBI double giving the Cubs an early 1-0 lead. *AP Photo*

never looking back.

But not even the growing legend of Kyle Schwarber could overshadow Cubs starter Jake Arrieta's run at the second no-hitter in World Series history.

"Yeah, I knew that I hadn't given up a hit all the way to the sixth," Arrieta said. "That's really not the focus in a game like this. I wanted to stay aggressive."

Arrieta, who pitched two no-hitters in the last

14 months, chased Don Larsen into the sixth inning before Glenbrook North's Jason Kipnis broke up the bid with a one-out double to center.

Larsen's 1956 perfect game for the Yankees remains the only no-hitter in the World Series.

"He did what he needed to do," said Kris Bryant, who singled and scored on Anthony Rizzo's ensuing double for the quick first-inning run. "It felt like a must-win for us. You don't want to go home down two games."

Arrieta didn't last long after the hit. After Kipnis took second on a grounder, he scored on a wild pitch. When Mike Napoli followed with a single to left, manager Joe Maddon lifted Arrieta in favor of lefty Mike Montgomery – who pitched two scoreless innings to get the ball to closer Aroldis Chapman.

As the Cubs head home for three games, the biggest question facing Maddon and the front office is how to get Schwarber involved.

The young lefty slugger just two games removed from 6½ months on the disabled list with a knee injury has reached base five times in nine plate appearances as the Cubs' designated hitter.

Medically cleared a week ago Monday to bat and run the bases, Schwarber has not been cleared to play in the field.

"Obviously, he looks good," Maddon said. "But that's something I'm waiting to hear from our medical side."

Teammates across the clubhouse said they wouldn't be surprised to see him in the outfield for the start of Friday's game – a scene that figures to only heighten what might already be the most emotionally charged game in Wrigley Field history.

"It's going to be insane," Rizzo said. "It's going to be a lot of emotions for a lot of people.

"It's a race to three now. We've got three games at home. We feel good about Friday night at Wrigley Field, Chicago, first World Series in 71 years. We're going to like the energy."

And two games into this series, on this stage, even the young, first-time players seem to have found their emotional footing as it shifts to a best-of-five.

"I felt like even today before the game, we were relaxed, having a good time, like we always do," Rizzo said.

The Cubs started a World Series-record six players under the age of 25.

"They're just scratching the surface of how good they can be," Maddon said.■

BOX SCORE

	1	2	3	4	5	6	7	8	9		R	H	E
Chicago	1	0	1	0	3	0	0	0	0		5	9	0
Cleveland	0	0	0	0	0	1	0	0	0		1	4	2

Cubs	AB	R	H	RBI	BB	SO	AVG.
Fowler CF	5	0	1	0	0	2	.111
Bryant 3B	5	1	1	0	0	1	.125
Rizzo 1B	3	2	1	1	2	0	.143
Zobrist LF	4	1	2	1	1	0	.625
Schwarber DH	4	1	2	2	1	2	.429
Báez 2B	5	0	1	0	0	2	.222
Contreras C	3	0	0	0	2	0	.200
Soler RF	2	0	0	0	1	0	.000
Heyward PR-RF	2	0	0	0	0	1	.000
Russell SS	4	0	1	1	1	0	.125
Totals	37	5	9	5	8	8	

Indians	AB	R	H	RBI	BB	SO	AVG.
Santana DH	4	0	0	0	0	2	.000
Kipnis 2B	4	1	1	0	0	2	.111
Lindor SS	3	0	0	0	1	1	.429
Napoli 1B	3	0	2	0	1	0	.333
Ramírez 3B	3	0	0	0	1	1	.429
Chisenhall RF	2	0	0	0	0	0	.167
Davis PH-CF	2	0	0	0	0	2	.143
Crisp LF	4	0	0	0	0	1	.000
Naquin CF	2	0	0	0	0	2	.000
Guyer PH-RF	1	0	1	0	1	0	.333
Pérez C	3	0	0	0	1	1	.286
Totals	31	1	4	0	5	12	

Cubs	IP	H	R	ER	BB	SO	HR	ERA
Arrieta (W, 1-0)	5.2	2	1	1	3	6	0	1.59
Montgomery	2.0	2	0	0	1	4	0	0.00
Chapman	1.1	0	0	0	1	2	0	0.00
Totals	9.0	4	1	1	5	12	0	

Indians	IP	H	R	ER	BB	SO	HR	ERA
Bauer (L, 0-1)	3.2	6	2	2	2	2	0	4.91
McAllister	0.2	1	2	2	1	2	0	27.00
Shaw	0.2	1	1	0	2	2	0	0.00
Salazar	1.0	0	0	0	2	0	0	0.00
Manship	0.1	1	0	0	1	0	0	0.00
Otero	1.2	0	0	0	0	1	0	0.00
Clevinger	1.0	0	0	0	0	1	0	0.00
Totals	9.0	9	5	4	8	8	0	

Cubs Dexter Fowler and Anthony Rizzo can only watch from the dugout during the ninth inning of Game 3. *AP Photo*

Cubs Bats Take Another Hiatus

Indians pinch-hitter Coco Crisp delivers a seventh inning RBI-single. *AP Photo*

by GORDON WITTENMYER

The World Series finally returned to Wrigley Field on Friday night, about 12 hours and a few hundreds of kegs behind the daylong celebration in the streets and establishments around the ballpark.

And, apparently, at least nine innings too early for the Cubs' bats.

Whether it was the "electric" atmosphere surrounding the first World Series game at Wrigley field in 71 years – fans cramming every nook of the ballpark and cranny at the corner of Clark and Addison – the Cubs were shut out for the fourth time this postseason.

Their 1-0 loss to the Cleveland Indians in Game 3 on Friday night might have been the least likely of the four.

"All the things adding up were like negatives to it," said first baseman Anthony Rizzo, who opened the ninth with a single to start a rally that fell 90 feet short of tying it. "Fly ball pitcher,

WORLD SERIES CHAMPIONS

101

Cubs right-fielder Jorge Soler delivers a seventh inning triple. Soler had two of the Cubs five hits on the day. *AP Photo*

wind's howling out [to left], it's October. So of course, it's a 1-0 game, with a broken bat to win it."

That was pinch-hitter Coco Crisp's one-out single to right in the seventh off rookie Carl Edwards Jr., to drive home Michael Martinez from third base.

"'Cleveland against the world' — that's kind of been our motto," said Crisp, who was reacquired

by his original team in a trade from Oakland over the summer. "Coming here and seeing all the blue in the stands and all the [Cubs] blue that was at our ballpark, you know the support for the Cubs is worldwide. You know what you're dealing with coming into the game."

How could anybody within a half-mile not feel the emotions pouring forth for blocks in either direction of Wrigley Field from early in the

CHICAGO CUBS

The Cubs Kris Bryant is forced out at second by Indians shortstop Francisco Lindor trying to advance on a ball hit by teammate Ben Zobrist during the fourth inning. *AP Photo*

BOX SCORE

	1	2	3	4	5	6	7	8	9		R	H	E
Cleveland	0	0	0	0	0	0	1	0	0		1	8	1
Chicago	0	0	0	0	0	0	0	0	0		0	5	0

Indians	AB	R	H	RBI	BB	SO	AVG.
Santana LF	1	0	0	0	2	1	.000
Miller P	0	0	0	0	0	0	.000
Crisp PH	1	0	1	1	0	0	.200
Shaw P	0	0	0	0	0	0	.000
Guyer LF	0	0	0	0	0	0	.333
Kipnis 2B	3	0	1	0	0	1	.167
Lindor SS	4	0	2	0	0	0	.455
Napoli 1B	4	0	0	0	0	3	.200
Ramírez 3B	4	0	2	0	0	0	.455
Allen P	0	0	0	0	0	0	.000
Chisenhall RF	4	0	0	0	0	2	.100
Pérez C	3	0	1	0	0	1	.300
Martínez PR-CF-3B	1	1	0	0	0	1	.000
Naquin CF	2	0	1	0	0	0	.250
Gomes C	1	0	0	0	0	0	.000
Tomlin P	1	0	0	0	0	1	.000
Davis LF-CF	0	0	0	0	1	0	.143
Totals	29	1	8	1	3	10	

Cubs	AB	R	H	RBI	BB	SO	AVG.
Fowler CF	4	0	1	0	0	1	.154
Bryant 3B	3	0	0	0	1	2	.091
Rizzo 1B	4	0	1	0	0	1	.182
2-Coghlan PR	0	0	0	0	0	0	.000
Zobrist LF	4	0	1	0	0	1	.500
Contreras C	4	0	0	0	0	0	.111
Soler RF	3	0	2	0	0	1	.400
1-Heyward PR-RF	1	0	0	0	0	0	.000
Báez 2B	4	0	0	0	0	1	.154
Russell SS	3	0	0	0	0	1	.091
Hendricks P	1	0	0	0	0	0	.000
Grimm P	0	0	0	0	0	0	.000
a-Montero PH	1	0	0	0	0	0	.000
Edwards Jr. P	0	0	0	0	0	0	.000
Montgomery P	0	0	0	0	0	0	.000
Strop P	0	0	0	0	0	0	.000
b-Schwarber PH	1	0	0	0	0	0	.375
Chapman P	0	0	0	0	0	0	.000
Totals	33	0	5	0	1	8	

Indians	IP	H	R	ER	BB	SO	HR	ERA
Tomlin	4.2	2	0	0	1	1	0	0.00
Miller (W, 1-0)	1.1	0	0	0	0	3	0	0.00
Shaw (H, 1)	1.2	2	0	0	0	1	0	0.00
Allen (S, 1)	1.1	1	0	0	0	3	0	0.00
Totals	9.0	5	0	0	1	8	0	

Cubs	IP	H	R	ER	BB	SO	HR	ERA
Hendricks	4.1	6	0	0	2	6	0	0.00
Grimm	0.2	0	0	0	0	0	0	10.80
Edwards Jr. (L, 0-1)	1.2	2	1	1	1	1	0	5.40
Montgomery	0.2	0	0	0	0	0	0	0.00
Strop	0.2	0	0	0	0	1	0	0.00
Chapman	1.0	0	0	0	0	2	0	0.00
Totals	9.0	8	1	1	3	10	0	

morning through the final pitch of the night?

The Cubs certainly did.

"We were so anxious to win this game that we tried to do too much," rookie catcher Willson Contreras said. "We were first-pitch swinging. We didn't see a lot of pitches.

"We were trying to do too much to [Indians starter Josh] Tomlin, and he made the right pitch in the right spots."

The Cubs' best chances to score came in the seventh and ninth, when the Cubs put men at third, each time with two out — each time with Javy Baez ending the inning.

In the seventh, Jorge Soler hit a two-out fly near the padded side wall in left that went for a triple when right-fielder Lonnie Chisenhall made an awkward leap for it, only to have it carom and roll past him. But Bryan Shaw induced an inning-ending grounder from Baez.

After Rizzo's single in the ninth, pinch-runner Chris Coghlan took second on a one-out grounder, then third when Jason Heyward drove a chopper off first baseman Mike Napoli for an error. After a stolen base put the Cubs in position to win with a hit, Baez struck out.

"We knew it wasn't going to be easy," said Rizzo, whose Cubs face a 2-1 deficit in a best-of-seven series for the second straight time in the postseason. "We've been in this situation before, last series, and we've just got to come back and do what we do."

If the Cubs thought getting back to the World Series for the first time in 71 years was tough, beating the Indians to win it has proved to be even harder.■

Indians pitcher Corey Kluber is safe at first as Cubs first baseman Anthony Rizzo is unable to catch the wide throw from third baseman Kris Bryant. *AP Photo*

World Series

GAME 4   OCTOBER 29, 2016   WRIGLEY FIELD   CHICAGO, ILLINOIS

CHICAGO CUBS 2   •   CLEVELAND INDIANS 7

Kluber Does It Again

Indians starting pitcher Corey Kluber improved to 4-1 with a 0.89 ERA in five playoff starts this year. *AP Photo*

by GORDON WITTENMYER

After 71 years of anticipation, it took just two nights of peculiar, exhilarating emotions at Wrigley Field to be reduced to a much more familiar feeling.

Wait till next year.

The Cubs weren't officially eliminated Saturday night in their first World Series since 1945. But Corey Kluber and the Indians turned the party

WORLD SERIES CHAMPIONS

105

Cubs center fielder Dexter Fowler hits a solo home run in the 8th inning. Fowler also doubled earlier in the game. *AP Photo*

in the streets outside the ballpark into a Sunday morning hangover with their 7-2 victory over the Cubs in Game 4.

Kluber pitched six shutdown innings against the Cubs for the second time five days, giving the Indians a 3-1 lead in the best-of-seven series and pushing the Cubs to the brink of elimination for the first time this postseason.

"It's a seven-game series, and we've played four games," said third baseman Kris Bryant, whose two throwing errors and three hitless at-bats were emblematic of the Cubs Saturday. "We're not out until we're out."

"We made mistakes tonight," Cubs manager Joe Maddon said, referring to Bryant's errors and an awkward throw by pitcher Mike Montgomery during an Indians rally in the sixth. "That was part of it. But then again, we have to do more offensively to give ourselves a chance."

More than 12-for-66 (.182) with 16 strikeouts in two nights. More than 1-for-14 with men in scoring position – more than three runs in 18 innings.

And less of the anxiousness and pressing young players such as Willson Contreras and Javy Baez admitted to during this woebegone trip home.

"It's the atmosphere of us wanting to do so much for these fans," veteran catcher David Ross said. "I think that's where it comes from.

"I don't know if there's a way to fix it," he added, "but I know the good news is we get to play

A dejected Chicago Cubs fan watches during the eighth inning of Game 4.
AP Photo

game 5 of the World Series tomorrow. There are worse places to be than Wrigley Field in Game 5 of the World Series."

World Series veteran John Lackey – the right-hander signed as a free agent last winter to pitch in October – had the best of three postseason starts, but lasted just five innings and trailed 3-1 to the Indians and their 2014 Cy Young winner.

Lackey retired the final eight batters he faced (for nine outs), but a home run and a throwing error led to a pair of Cleveland runs in the second, and a leadoff double in the third led to another.

Meanwhile, the Cubs jumped on Kluber for a quick run in the first. But Kluber, pitching on short rest, gave up only two more singles through five, left Rizzo at second after a leadoff single in the sixth, and improved to 4-1 with a 0.75 ERA in five

starts this postseason – 2-0 with one run in 12 innings against the Cubs.

By the time the time Dexter Fowler homered off Andrew Miller in the eighth for the Cubs' other run, Glenbrook North grad Jason Kipnis had tacked on a three-run homer off Travis Wood in the seventh – part of a three-hit night that included that double in the third and earned him boos from his hometown by his final at-bat.

The good news for the Cubs is they don't have to face Kluber Sunday, or even Tuesday in Cleveland if Lester beats Game 2 loser Trevor Bauer.

The bad news: Kluber is lying in the weeds for a possible Game 7 start, on three days' rest again.■

Cubs third baseman Kris Bryant connects for a home run to spark a three run fourth inning rally. *AP Photo*

Cubs Stay Alive – Head Back To Cleveland

Cubs relief pitcher Aroldis Chapman came on in the seventh inning and recorded the first eight-out save of his big league career.
AP Photo

by GORDON WITTENMYER

It took three tries – and nearly three innings from their closer – but the Cubs won a World Series game at Wrigley Field for the first time in 71 years Sunday night.

Just in time to win an all-expenses-paid return trip to Cleveland with their season alive, if not kicking, after a 3-2 nail-biter over the Indians in Game 5.

Cubs postseason ace Jon Lester started this must-win game, but the pitching story of survival on this night was the biggest – and longest – save of Aroldis Chapman's career.

Cubs catcher David Ross and first baseman Anthony Rizzo team up to catch a foul ball hit by the Indians Carlos Santana during the second inning. *AP Photo*

The left-hander acquired from the Yankees at the trade deadline retired eight of the final 10 Indians batters of the game, four on strikeouts, to nurse a one-run lead all the way to the shores of Lake Erie.

"Gutsy," teammate Anthony Rizzo called it. "He told me it's big cajones."

The only thing bigger might have been the magnitude of the Cubs first actual must-win game of the year an elimination game created by back-to-back, low-wattage losses to the Indians Friday and Saturday.

"It's awesome. But we've still got some work to do," leadoff man Dexter Fowler said. "We've got two more games."

"Why not us?" said MVP favorite Kris Bryant, whose leadoff homer in the fourth tied the game Sunday and opened the decisive, three-run rally. "I feel like we play our best with our backs up against the wall.

"Hopefully, we can get out there and win Game 6, because you never know what can happen in Game 7," Bryant added.

The Cubs scored only once in their final game of the year at Wrigley Field, but the three runs in the fourth were enough for this win – and more than they had scored in the previous two games combined.

After the Indians closed to within a run on Francsico Lindor's two-out RBI single in the sixth, Joe Maddon got as aggressive as he has in two years managing the Cubs.

He pinch-hit lefty hitting catcher Miguel Montero for starter David Ross with two out and nobody on in the bottom of the sixth.

And after Montero struck out to end the inning, he emptied his bench of able-bodied catchers by sending rookie Willson Contreras into the game to

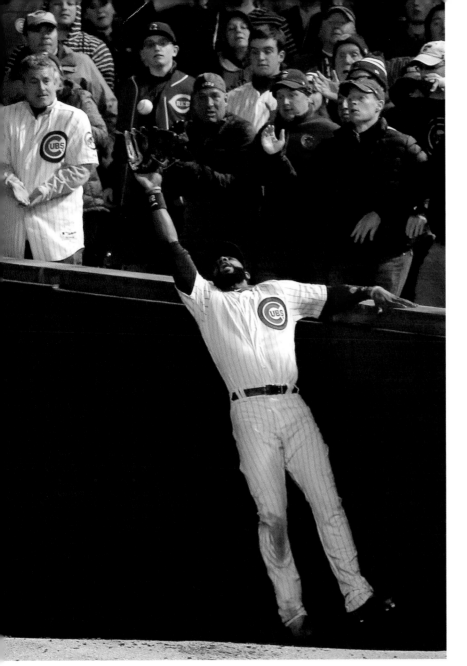

Cubs right fielder Jason Heyward makes a great catch on a foul ball hit by Indians pitcher Trevor Bauer during the third inning. *AP Photo*

BOX SCORE

	1	2	3	4	5	6	7	8	9		R	H	E
Cleveland	0	1	0	0	0	1	0	0	0		2	6	1
Chicago	0	0	0	3	0	0	0	0	-		3	7	0

Indians	AB	R	H	RBI	BB	SO	AVG.
Davis CF	4	1	2	0	0	1	.200
Kipnis 2B	4	0	0	0	0	2	.238
Lindor SS	4	0	1	1	0	2	.421
Napoli 1B	4	0	1	0	0	0	.200
Santana LF	4	0	1	0	0	0	.267
Ramírez 3B	4	1	1	1	0	2	.300
Guyer RF	2	0	0	0	0	1	.143
Pérez C	3	0	0	0	0	0	.188
Allen P	0	0	0	0	0	0	.000
Bauer P	1	0	0	0	0	0	.000
Clevinger P	0	0	0	0	0	0	.000
Crisp PH	1	0	0	0	0	0	.286
Shaw P	0	0	0	0	0	0	.000
Gomes C	1	0	0	0	0	1	.000
Totals	32	2	6	2	0	9	

Cubs	AB	R	H	RBI	BB	SO	AVG.
Fowler CF	3	0	0	0	0	1	.200
Bryant 3B	3	1	1	1	1	2	.118
Rizzo 1B	3	1	1	0	1	0	.294
Zobrist LF	3	1	1	0	1	0	.368
Russell SS	4	0	2	1	0	1	.211
Heyward RF	4	0	1	0	0	3	.273
Báez 2B	4	0	1	0	0	3	.143
Ross C	1	0	0	1	0	0	.250
Montero PH	1	0	0	0	0	1	.000
Edwards Jr. P	0	0	0	0	0	0	.000
Chapman P	1	0	0	0	0	1	.000
Lester P	2	0	0	0	0	2	.000
Contreras C	1	0	0	0	0	0	.071
Totals	30	3	7	3	3	14	

Indians	IP	H	R	ER	BB	SO	HR	ERA
Bauer (L, 0-2)	4.0	6	3	3	0	7	1	5.87
Clevinger	1.0	0	0	0	2	0	0	0.00
Shaw	1.1	0	0	0	0	3	0	0.00
Allen	1.2	1	0	0	1	4	0	0.00
Totals	8.0	7	3	3	3	14	1	

Cubs	IP	H	R	ER	BB	SO	HR	ERA
Lester (W, 1-1)	6.0	4	2	2	0	5	1	3.86
Edwards Jr. (H, 1)	0.1	1	0	0	0	0	0	4.50
Chapman (S, 1)	2.2	1	0	0	0	4	0	0.00
Totals	9.0	6	2	2	0	9	1	

catch rookie Carl Edwards Jr. on a double switch to start the top of the seventh – pulling Lester at 90 pitches with a 3-2 lead in his last game of the season, win or lose.

Edwards immediately gave up a leadoff single to Mike Napoli, followed by a passed ball by Contreras to put the potential tying run in scoring position with nobody out.

Then as soon as Edwards got Carlos Santana to fly to left for the first out, Maddon pulled a Terry Francona and went to closer Aroldis Chapman for the would-be eight-out save.

It was the first time Chapman had been used as early as the seventh inning since he became a regular closer in May 2012. It turned into the longest outing of his career by a third of an inning.

The only runners he allowed were on a two-out hit batter in the seventh and a one-out single in the eighth that would have been an out if he had covered first on Rizzo's diving stop.

Instead Rajai Davis stole second and third, threatening to tie the game – before Chapman struck out Lindor with a 101-mph fastball to leave him there.

"We've got to go on another one-game win streak," Rizzo said. "We're obviously happy right now, but we've got to gear it up for Tuesday." ∎

Cubs reliever Travis Wood and catcher Willson Contreras celebrate the Game 6 win. *AP Photo*

World Series

GAME 6   NOVEMBER 1, 2016   PROGRESSIVE FIELD   CLEVELAND, OHIO

CHICAGO CUBS 9 • CLEVELAND INDIANS 3

Cubs Rout Indians to Force Game 7

Chicago Cubs first baseman Anthony Rizzo (left), along with teammates Ben Zobrist and Kyle Schwarber celebrate Addison Russell's third inning grand slam.   *AP Photo*

by GORDON WITTENMYER

After 108 years, two weeks and four days, it has all come down to this for these Cubs who would write their own history:

A Game 7 appearance almost as rare as the championship itself.

A record-setting performance by the youngest Cub on the field, and a 97-mph pitching start by

the baddest, gave the Cubs a 9-3 victory over the Cleveland Indians in Game 6 of the World Series and assured that November 2 will be a date long remembered by one of these star-crossed franchises.

"It's just correct and apt that we'd go seven games," said manager Joe Maddon, who brought

WORLD SERIES CHAMPIONS

113

Umpire Joe West looks on as Cubs left fielder Ben Zobrist collides with Indians catcher Roberto Perez as he scores during the first inning of Game 6. *AP Photo*

Cubs MVP candidate Kris Bryant drills a first-inning home run off of Indians starting pitcher Josh Tomlin. Bryant would end up with four hits on the night. *AP Photo*

his closer, Aroldis Chapman, into the game in the seventh inning for the second elimination game in a row.

Shortstop Addison Russell, 22, hit the first Cubs grand slam in World Series history, and starter Jake Arrieta was powerful again into the sixth to become the first since Bob Gibson to win two road starts in a World Series.

But it will be what comes next that will make the history these guys keep talking about writing.

After 209 games from March through the six-month season and a month of playoffs, every

target they embraced, every ghost they dismissed, every reason all those free agents took less money to sign comes down to one night in Cleveland in November.

It's the third Game 7 in franchise history. Both of the others were losses, most recently in the 2003 National League Championship Series against the Marlins; the other was the last time the Cubs reached the World Series, in 1945 against the Tigers.

"I don't even think we're really thinking about that," Russell said. "A lot of us are going into

	1	2	3	4	5	6	7	8	9		R	H	E
Chicago	3	0	4	0	0	0	0	0	2		9	13	0
Cleveland	0	0	0	1	1	0	0	0	1		3	6	1

Cubs	AB	R	H	RBI	BB	SO	AVG.
Fowler CF	5	0	0	0	0	1	.160
Schwarber DH	4	1	1	0	1	0	.333
Bryant 3B	5	2	4	1	0	0	.273
Rizzo 1B	5	3	3	2	0	0	.364
Zobrist LF	4	2	2	0	1	1	.391
Russell SS	5	1	2	6	0	1	.250
Contreras C	3	0	0	0	1	1	.059
Heyward RF	4	0	0	0	0	0	.200
Báez 2B	4	0	1	0	0	2	.160
Totals	39	9	13	9	3	6	

Indians	AB	R	H	RBI	BB	SO	AVG.
Santana DH	4	0	0	0	1	1	.211
Kipnis 2B	5	2	3	1	0	0	.308
Lindor SS	3	0	0	0	1	1	.364
Napoli 1B	4	0	1	1	0	3	.211
Ramírez 3B	4	0	1	0	0	1	.292
Chisenhall RF	1	0	0	0	1	1	.071
Gomes PH	1	0	0	0	0	0	.000
Martínez RF	0	0	0	0	0	0	.000
Crisp LF	1	0	0	0	1	0	.250
Guyer PH-LF	1	1	0	0	1	0	.125
Naquin CF	2	0	0	0	0	2	.143
Davis PH-CF	2	0	0	0	0	0	.176
Pérez C	3	0	1	1	1	1	.211
Totals	31	3	6	3	6	10	

Cubs	IP	H	R	ER	BB	SO	HR	ERA
Arrieta (W, 2-0)	5.2	3	2	2	3	9	1	2.38
Montgomery	1.0	1	0	0	1	0	0	2.08
Chapman	1.1	1	1	1	0	1	0	1.42
Strop	0.2	1	0	0	1	0	0	0.00
Wood	0.1	0	0	0	0	0	0	5.40
Totals	9.0	6	3	3	6	10	1	

Indians	IP	H	R	ER	BB	SO	HR	ERA
Tomlin (L, 0-1)	2.1	6	6	6	1	0	1	7.71
Otero	0.2	1	1	1	0	0	1	2.70
Salazar	2.0	1	0	0	0	4	0	0.00
Manship	0.2	1	0	0	0	1	0	0.00
McAllister	1.1	2	0	0	0	0	0	9.00
Clevinger	2.0	2	2	2	2	1	1	4.50
Totals	9.0	13	9	9	3	6	3	

Cubs starting pitcher, Jake Arrieta, had a strong outing with nine strikeouts in Game 6.   *AP Photo*

tomorrow thinking it's just another game."

Of course, it's not just another game. Just ask the only player in the Cubs' clubhouse who has played a Game 7 – 2002 Game 7 starter John Lackey.

"People that try to tell you it's just another game are lying to you," Lackey said. "There's going to be some different emotions. You've got to embrace that. Don't fight it. You just try to use those and channel them in the right direction."

For the Cubs to win their third World Series title, first since 1908, they have to beat former Cy Young winner Corey Kluber for the first time after losing Games 1 and 4 to him. Kluber is pitching on short rest for the second consecutive start.

The Cubs counter with Kyle Hendricks, who went from fifth starter to leading the majors in ERA in the span of six months this season.

If the Cubs win Wednesday, they'll become the sixth team to come back from a 3-1 deficit in the World Series to win.

"Anybody who plays this game grows up dreaming of winning a World Series," said Kris Bryant, whose four-hit night included a first-inning homer. "We get to play in a Game 7. That's pretty special.

"But we can't get too far ahead of ourselves. When we were down 3-1, it was take it a game at a time and try to get to Game 7," he added. "[Wednesday] we're going to be there, and it's nice to kind of build off of these last two games with momentum."

Arrieta pitched two outs deep into the sixth in another strong start in Cleveland, retiring nine of the first 10 he faced, and beating the Indians for the second time this series.

If you didn't know what the adrenaline and emotions of a second straight elimination game would do for the Cubs' 2015 Cy Young Award winner, consider Arrieta's fastball reached 97 mph Tuesday night – his top velocity of the year.∎

WORLD SERIES CHAMPIONS

Progressive Field,
World Series Game 7.
AP Photo

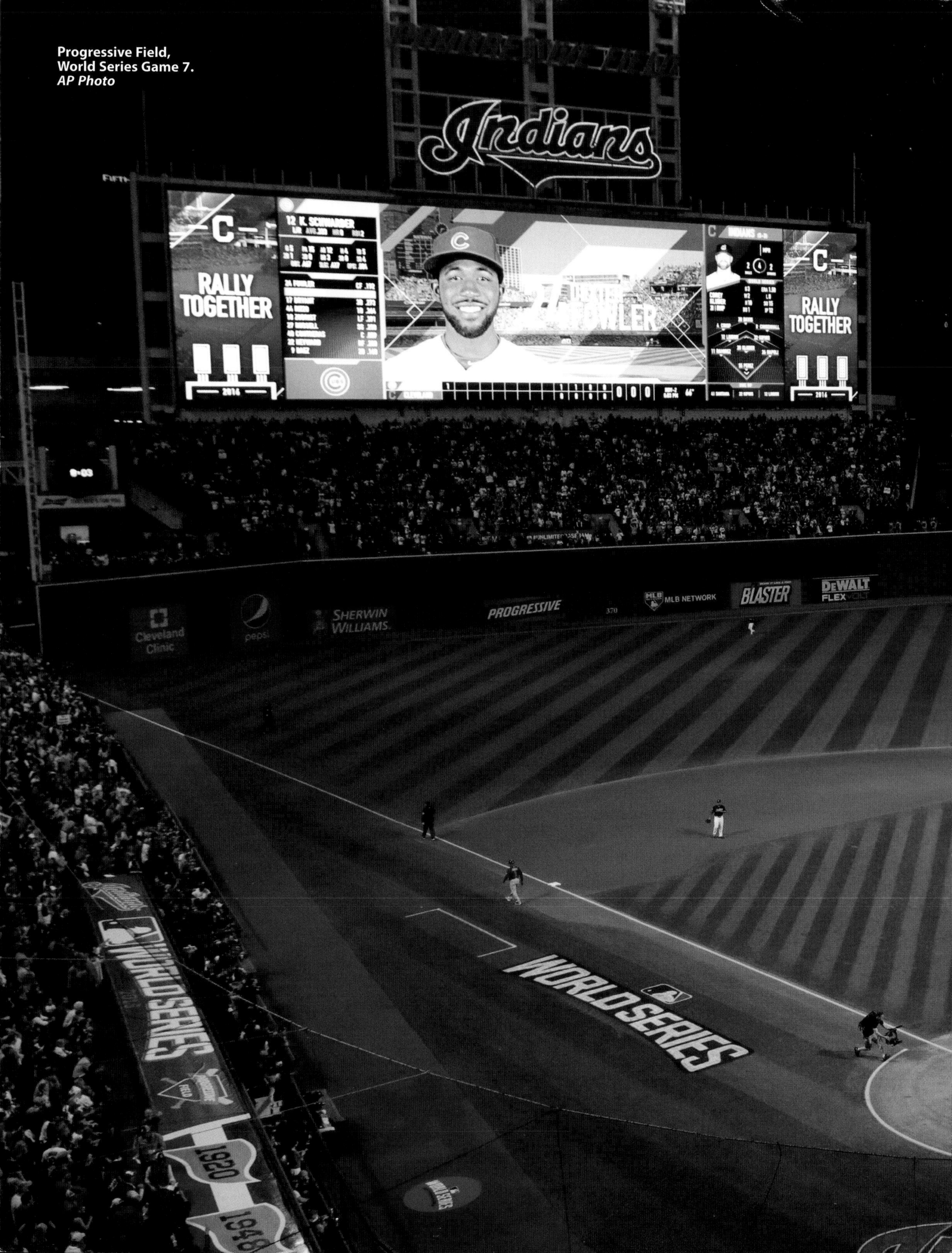

Cubs first baseman Anthony Rizzo reacts after teammate Kris Bryant scored on Rizzo's hit during the fifth inning. *AP Photo*

World Series

CHICAGO CUBS 8 • CLEVELAND INDIANS 7

After 108 Years
Cubs Win World Series!

Cubs center fielder Dexter Fowler celebrates his lead off home run as the Cubs dugout erupts in the top of the first inning.
AP Photo

by GORDON WITTENMYER

When Kris Bryant's throw to first was safely in the glove of Anthony Rizzo in the bottom of the 10th inning, it was finally over.

An 8-7, extra-inning victory over the Indians on the road in Game 7 of the World Series finally ended – and finally put an end to more than a century of misery and mockery.

Go ahead and run down the list of all the presidents that have come and gone, the world wars that have been fought and won, the states

WORLD SERIES CHAMPIONS

Cubs third baseman Kris Bryant slides in safe at home as Indians catcher Roberto Perez puts on a late tag during the fourth inning. *AP Photo*

Ben Zobrist lines an RBI double to left in the top of the 10th inning giving the Cubs the lead. *AP Photo*

that have entered the union and the countless tears, heartache and hopelessness generated in Chicago for 108 years of Cubs baseball.

Just know this: For all who have waited and yearned, this one, long, wet night in November in Cleveland was nothing short of the best thing since 20 years before sliced bread.

That's really how long it's been since Frank Chance and the boys beat the Tigers in 1908 and started making space in their parlors for all the trophies that seemed sure to follow.

"It's fitting it has to be done with one of the best games of all-time," said team president Theo Epstein, who now has presided over the ends of the two most storied "curses" in major league history – having been the general manager in Boston 12 years ago when the Red Sox ended the

86-year "Curse of the Bambino."

"What a testament to our players," Epstein said. "During the rain delay they said, 'this is only going to make it sweeter, boys.' Our fans deserve this so much – and all the former Cubs. This is for Ernie Banks, Billy Williams and Ron Santo."

Joe Maddon's boys needed to survive their manager's heavily scripted pitching machinations, a three-run rally in the eighth by the Indians against a gassed Aroldis Chapman that sent the game to extra innings, and to endure a brief rain delay before the 10th.

But when veterans Ben Zobrist and Miguel Montero delivered RBI hits in the 10th, the surprisingly Chicago-strong crowd at Progressive Field started the roar.

"I know he [Bryan Shaw] throws a hard cutter,"

Cubs first baseman Anthony Rizzo raises his arms triumphantly after catching third baseman Kris Bryant's throw for the final out of Game 7. *AP Photo*

said Zobrist, who won his second consecutive ring – and this year's World Series MVP award. "I was just battling."

And when Mike Montgomery got the final out to quell another Indians rally in the bottom of the 10th, the Cubs started the party more than a century in the making.

Thousands of Cubs fans remained well after the game, waving `W' flags and serenading the players on the field with what certainly was the loudest rendition of "Go Cubs Go" performed east of Lake Michigan.

Then some of the players hoisted retiring veteran clubhouse leader David Ross onto their shoulders for a ride to the dugout, to a huge ovation.

Ross, of course, hit one of the Cubs' three homers in their first Game 7 postseason win in three tries.

"A lot of ups and downs. I'm totally exhausted," Ross said. "These guys are winners. When you want to crumble, when ball goes over the fence [in the Indians' eighth], these guys keep battling back."

These new-age Cubs pulled this all off by coming back from the brink of elimination to win three straight games an epic seven-game Series, becoming the first team since the Royals in 1985 to come back from a 3-1 deficit to win the World Series – first since the 1979 Pirates to do it on the road.

"We started as heavy favorites and we went wire to wire," Rizzo said. "We were written off [down 3-1] and to come back is the best feeling in the world."

They trailed 1-0 in Game 5 on Sunday at home when National League MVP favorite Kris Bryant homered leading off the fourth inning.

The World Series champion Cubs celebrate on the field and in the locker room following Game 7.   *AP Photo*

Cubs catcher David Ross is carried off the field by his teammates following Game 7. Ross hit a home run in his only at bat of the game. *AP Photo*

BOX SCORE

	1	2	3	4	5	6	7	8	9	10	R	H	E
Chicago	1	0	0	2	2	1	0	0	0	2	8	13	3
Cleveland	0	0	1	0	2	0	0	3	0	1	7	11	1

Cubs	AB	R	H	RBI	BB	SO	AVG.
Fowler CF	5	1	3	1	0	0	.233
Schwarber DH	5	0	3	0	0	0	.412
Almora Jr. PR-DH	0	1	0	0	0	0	.000
Bryant 3B	4	2	1	0	1	1	.269
Rizzo 1B	3	1	1	1	1	1	.360
Zobrist LF	5	1	1	1	0	0	.357
Russell SS	3	0	0	1	1	0	.222
Contreras C	2	0	1	1	0	0	.105
Ross C	1	1	1	1	1	0	.400
Coghlan PR	0	0	0	0	0	0	.000
Montero C	1	0	1	1	0	0	.250
Heyward RF	5	0	0	0	0	1	.150
Báez 2B	5	1	1	1	0	2	.167
Totals	39	8	13	8	4	5	

Indians	AB	R	H	RBI	BB	SO	AVG.
Santana DH	4	1	1	1	1	0	.217
Kipnis 2B	5	1	1	0	0	3	.290
Lindor SS	5	0	0	0	0	1	.296
Napoli 1B	5	0	0	0	0	3	.167
Ramírez 3B	5	1	2	0	0	0	.310
Chisenhall RF	2	0	1	0	0	0	.125
Guyer PH-RF-LF	2	2	2	1	1	0	.300
Davis CF	5	1	2	3	0	0	.227
Crisp LF	4	1	1	0	0	0	.333
Martínez RF	1	0	0	0	0	0	.000
Pérez C	1	0	0	0	1	1	.200
Naquin PR	0	0	0	0	0	0	.143
Gomes C	1	0	0	0	0	1	.000
Totals	40	7	11	5	3	9	

Cubs	IP	H	R	ER	BB	SO	HR	ERA
Hendricks	4.2	4	2	1	1	2	0	1.00
Lester	3.0	3	2	1	1	4	0	3.68
Chapman (W, 1-0; B, 1)	1.1	3	2	2	0	2	1	3.52
Edwards Jr. (H, 2)	0.2	1	1	1	1	1	0	6.75
Montgomery (S, 1)	0.1	0	0	0	0	0	0	1.9
Totals	10.0	11	7	5	3	9	1	

Indians	IP	H	R	ER	BB	SO	HR	ERA
Kluber	4.0	6	4	4	0	0	2	2.81
Miller	2.1	4	2	2	1	1	1	3.52
Allen	2.0	0	0	0	1	2	0	0.00
Shaw (L, 0-1)	1.0	3	2	2	2	1	0	3.86
Bauer	0.2	0	0	0	0	1	0	5.40
Totals	10.0	13	8	8	4	5	3	

They scored twice more in that inning and never trailed again in the series – though it got a lot more complicated than that by the time manager Maddon watched his scripted-by-Hollywood pitching plans for the night blow up after pulling starter Kyle Hendricks with two out and a runner at first in the fifth, leading 4-1.

Maddon kicked most of his bullpen to the curb for the first nine innings Wednesday, sending starters Jon Lester, Jake Arrieta and John Lackey to the bullpen early in the game and, apparently, drooling for the chance to return to 100-mph closer Chapman for the finish.

In executing that plan, Maddon finally discovered the limits of the willing but far from sharp left-hander, costing the Cubs a chance for history in nine innings on this night.

He got three innings out of Game 5 winner Lester – swapping him and personal catcher Ross into the game for Hendricks and Willson Contreras with two out and one on in the fifth. It cost two quick runs on a Ross error and a two-run wild pitch before Lester settled in.

But he still took a 6-3 lead just four outs from the finish line before allowing an infield single and watching Maddon emerge from the dugout 55 pitches after handing him the ball.

Enter Chapman. Exit the Cubs' lead.

A ringing double by Brandon Guyer drove home one run, and after fouling off several pitches, Rajai Davis lined a 2-2 pitch from Chapman over the wall down the left-field line to tie.

After a scoreless ninth, the tarp was pulled onto the field for 17 minutes.

"We regrouped during the rain delay. Give our guys all the credit," Maddon said. "What a bunch of professionals. We never quit."■

WORLD SERIES CHAMPIONS

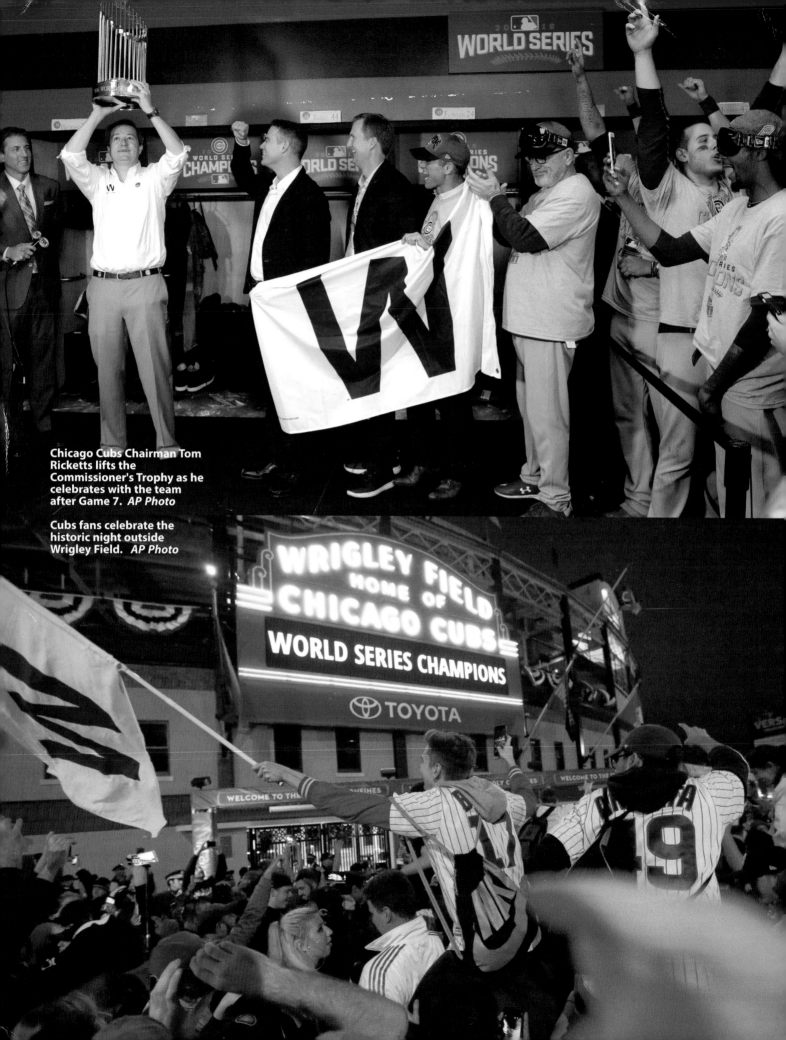

Chicago Cubs Chairman Tom Ricketts lifts the Commissioner's Trophy as he celebrates with the team after Game 7. *AP Photo*

Cubs fans celebrate the historic night outside Wrigley Field. *AP Photo*